Praying Peace

other books by James F. Twyman

published by Findhorn Press

The Secret of the Beloved Disciple

Portrait of the Master

published by Warner Books

Emissary of light

Praying Peace

James F. Twyman

In conversation with
Gregg Braden
and
Doreen Virtue

FINDHORN
Press

First published by Findhorn Press in 2000

ISBN 1-899171-48-7

British Library Cataloguing-in-Publication Data.
A catalogue record for this book is available from the British Library.

Library of Congress Catalog Card Number: 00-105097

Layout by Pam Bochel

Front cover design by Dale Vermeer
Back cover design by Thierry Bogliolo

Printed and bound in Canada

Published by
Findhorn Press

The Park, Findhorn   P.O. Box 13939
Forres IV36 3TY   Tallahassee
Scotland   Florida 32317-3939, USA
Tel 01309 690582   Tel 850 893 2920
Fax 01309 690036   Fax 850 893 3442

e-mail info@findhornpress.com
findhornpress.com

Contents

Section 1

Chapter One

Here's a question you've probably asked yourself before, one that is often heard in philosophical or spiritual circles. If you're optimistic, then you'll probably agree with the premise I'm about to suggest, while others will claim it is unrealistic at best. Until now the answer has been a matter of opinion, depending more on your point of view than provable fact. But sometimes the things that were considered yesterday's fantasy are today accepted as normal parts of our everyday lives. I believe that this question qualifies for the latter.

So here it is: "Can one person, properly motivated, change the world?" How many examples can you think of, people who have made critical contributions to science or world peace, on whom we look back and say, "Yes, that person really changed things." Everyone is entitled to their own personal hero and favorite, someone they hold up to the light that would otherwise expose common imperfections, someone who inspires us and gives the rest of us hope.

But what about you? It's one thing to look at Albert Einstein or Mahatma Gandhi and affirm such a statement, but it's quite another to think that you could make an equal impact, not necessarily in the public arena but in a way that is just as important. Do you have the 'stuff' to change the world, to shift the course of human evolution to the point that we are better off than we were before? Or are you just another face in the crowd, sailing along on the ship we call life to an uncertain destiny that you have no real way of influencing?

This is one of the big questions in life, and the goal of this book is to answer it once and for all. Do you have the power to change the world, to make an impact on the way that each one of us experiences who we are, or why we're here? The answer is YES! The truth, if you really want to be honest, is that you always have had the power. The decisions you have made have shaped every experience of the world you have ever had, every aspect of the life you live. What if you have more power within you than you can even imagine? What if you're not the weak, unimportant, insignificant person you thought you were? What would happen then?

The title of this book, *Praying Peace,* may make some of you a little uncomfortable. I personally have no problem with this since we sometimes need some discomfort to shake us free from the habitual patterns that have shaped our lives. Letting go of these habits can push us to the point of real transformation, and that, more than anything, is the purpose of this book. We hear words like *Prayer* and we immediately remember some painful experience in Sunday school like the time we were scolded for missing a word in the "Lord's Prayer." (I personally thought that God's real name was 'Howard' because of just such a misunderstanding... you know, "Our Father who art in Heaven, 'Howard' be thy name.") Or we hear the word *Peace* and we think about those well-intentioned marches in the 1960's when an entire generation chanted, "All we are saying..."

Maybe it's time to reframe these words in a way that empowers us beyond the normal bounds of religion or custom. Maybe *Prayer* means more than we thought it did, and *Peace* is more than just an idea, but has become a powerful reality.

So let's begin this process of discovery at once by defining two words that we'll come back to again and again – Prayer and Peace. I'll admit that it's almost impossible for words to communicate the subtle truths that would reveal the 'reality' we seek here. After all, words are really "symbols of symbols," as *A Course in Miracles* says, and are therefore "twice removed from the truth." What we're really after is the 'experience' behind the words, the 'feeling' that teaches us what mere words cannot. But for now, at least for the moment, we'll forgive such inadequacies and forge ahead, hoping that one or two of the words in this book will spark the memory of something more profound.

We'll define 'Prayer' as *Becoming Aware of the Awareness of God.* Let's stop there for a moment and really breathe this one in since the experience it is meant to evoke is so very important. First of all, what is the Awareness of God? However

11

we define the Ultimate Reality (otherwise known as God), we can probably agree that He/She/It is fully aware of us, all of us, all the time. This Infinite Mind is not limited by the distractions that so often steal our attention, but is always, in every way, focused on the truth within each one of us. We can even say that this is the greatest act of love, since we seem to find it so hard to focus on the truth within ourselves. God, then, is not fooled by the shifting, changing, mutable illusions that seem to rule our lives, but is the very constancy that defines what we'll call 'Reality.' And this Being, whoever it is, never forgets us even for an instant.

I remember when I was a freshman in high school, the Christian Brother who taught us Religion asked if it was possible for God to forget us. It must have sounded like a trick question to the rest of the class since I was the only one who had enough courage to raise my hand. "No, God cannot forget us," I said, "not even for a second." "Why?" the Brother asked me. "Because... because we would no longer exist." It sounded like a good answer at the time, and it apparently was enough to satisfy the teacher. In retrospect it would have been better to say, "We could have never come into existence if it was possible for God to forget us. Therefore, the fact that we exist at all, and are conscious of that existence, means that there is a God, and that God is always aware of us."

If this is true, then the next question is: "How do we become Aware of this Awareness?" Let's say that Awareness, in this sense, is communication. We cannot communicate with anyone unless we are aware of him or her. God is always aware of us, so the fact that we are not always aware of God means that we're the ones who have broken off communication. Becoming Aware of the Awareness of God is the act of reestablishing the flow of information between our Source and us. The word we are choosing to use to describe this experience is 'Prayer.'

Our second word, 'Peace,' is a little harder to define. I would begin by suggesting the words of St. Paul who referred to the "Peace that surpasseth understanding." It is hard, if not impossible, for us to imagine an experience without an opposite. If we hear that someone is good, then we immediately think of someone else who is bad. If we jump into the ocean and feel cold, our minds instantly remember a bathtub that was hot. We think in terms of contrast, as if life was a sliding scale that allows us to measure every experience against another seemingly opposite one.

'Peace,' then, is not the opposite of war, but an 'experience' that transcends all definitions, linking us to our eternal nature.

Is it possible for us to experience something that is so pure, so whole, that it cannot be compared to anything at all? Better yet, if we were able to have such an experience, do we have words to describe it? The answer to the first question is yes, and the answer to the second is no. It is indeed possible for us to enter into an experience that has no opposite, but only when we are willing to lay aside every judgment we have ever made about the world, about each other, and especially about ourselves. And yet, once we have entered into this sacred

13

chamber, words no longer work. Once again, words are symbols of symbols and can never describe what lies behind every symbol. "Of this we cannot speak," the mystics often say, for the experience of reality is beyond the comprehension of the rational mind.

'Peace', for our purposes, is the reality that lies behind every symbol, every word, and every attempt to define what has no definition. When we enter a state of communication with the Divine, or 'Prayer', then we are 'Aware of God', and we 'Experience Peace'. This is the basic formula employed by this book.

This being understood, how do we 'Pray Peace'? Is there a way for us to use this formula to make a real difference on the planet, creating a world based upon the laws of love?

In this era of technology and scientific discovery, we have been led to believe that strength and economic prowess define power. Some of us can remember the dawn of the atomic era when a weapon was developed, a single one of which could destroy an entire city. This, we were told, was power. Many more lived through a cold war based, not upon traditional weapons but on a chess-game of wits, with leaders who demonstrated courage and restraint in the face of possible global annihilation. Again, the world was led to believe that this was the essence of power. On the scientific front, discoveries were being made that made Newtonian physicists reassess their centuries' old version of natural law. This, after all, must be real power.

And yet, there is a power that is more ancient than all these discoveries, better proven that any scientific formula, and sometimes more disregarded than the notion of a flat earth. In our race to find a powerful universe, we have forgotten that the real power is within, the place where reality and actuality are born and where they live. After all, the world's great works of art, its fantastic structures and our remarkable achievements were not born from the mud and dirt, but within our minds. Each of these inspired legacies had a common source – they were born in a world that is invisible to the eye, but they then found their way into physicality and form. The real power, then, is not 'out there somewhere', but so close to who we are that we often forget to give credit where credit is due.

Most of you are willing to accept this statement as fact, and more than likely have already done so. The purpose of this book, however, is to go one step further, to see what lies behind this fabulous spirit of ours and discover the real source of creation. Some of us were raised to believe that prayer has the power to affect our lives, but were we taught that it is the very foundation of 'real' power, a creative force that can not only affect the world, but which actually made it? What if there is far more to our concepts of prayer than the formulas we were told to recite while kneeling beside our beds before going to sleep? What if there is a system, or an actual science, behind this mysterious veil and it has the power to change everything, especially our own lives? If that is true, if you have always had the key to unlimited peace, happiness and joy, then you'd better brace yourself because everything is about to change.

Stop for a moment and consider your own attitudes toward prayer. I personally feel very lucky to have been given a strong foundation by my parents and other teachers who instilled within me a great respect for this mysterious practice called prayer. I was raised with a strong Irish Catholic backbone and a propensity for all things mystical. Unlike many of my friends, I didn't need to be talked into going to church, I insisted on it. And though I was exposed to the same childish attitudes that some people complain about even when they become adults (especially when they become adults), I was somehow given the grace to see past these forms into something more essential, something that grabbed my attention from a very early age.

The rosary was my mantra, and I longed to participate in the magical rituals I saw the priest conducting on the altar. He might as well have been a wizard, and as soon as I was able, at the ripe age of eighteen, I left home to enter the hallowed institution that had reared me, the Church that breathed air into my lungs and gave me life.

Oh, would that it had been that simple! I was either too young to make such a commitment, or I intuitively knew that my destiny lay down a different path. I left the Franciscans after only a year and a half and began a much more ordinary existence. And yet the echo of those early years was never fully banished from my slightly soiled spirit, and before long I began searching for wisdom beyond the walls of my former cloister. Inquiries into other religions and other spiritual paths brought me the realization that we are all looking for the same thing – peace. It may be known by different names in different places, but ultimately, when you look beneath the trappings and dogmas of each religion, you find an unquenchable desire to experience the "peace that surpasseth understanding." This discovery turned my world upside down.

And so my path of prayer was set. I knew it was a powerful force, I just didn't know how powerful. I was like an athlete who pushes the limits of their body just to see how fast they can run; that's how determined I was to see if prayer could really change the world. People tried to tell me that prayer is just a passive, self-indulgent passion for the weak minded, or at best a sectarian approach to real spiritual growth, but something told me there was more to it. I began to suspect that there is a common thread that could pull us all together and change the way we think about each other, even about God and about ourselves. To me that thread became the peace prayers from the different religions of the world, and once I found them I held onto them like a drowning man holds onto a life raft.

In November 1986 something incredible happened in Assisi, Italy, the home of St. Francis. Pope John Paul II decided that it was time for the leaders of the twelve major religions of the world to come together to celebrate peace. What an idea! And each one of them brought a special gift to offer to the others, something that to my mind was more valuable than diamonds or gold. In a ceremony that may prove to be of

17

monumental importance in the centuries to come, each one of these spiritual masters prayed the prayer from their tradition that defined their own longing for peace. They prayed and they listened, and when all was said and done, there was one important realization – they all wanted the same thing. More than that, if you took certain definitive words like Allah, Buddha or Christ out of the prayers, it was hard to tell which prayer belonged to which religion. How brilliant! The world began to realize that we aren't so far apart after all. And the religions of the world, those very institutions that had often used faith in a loving God as the launch pad for intolerance and war, became the bright beacons that would initiate a new era of peace.

How could I have known that these prayers would define and activate my life? One day I was sitting in my room going through a drawer and I saw them there, on a sheet a friend had given to me and which I hadn't even taken the time to read. And yet at that moment I felt a pull, sort of a Divine lure, that forced me to read, then pick up the guitar that was leaning against the wall beside me. As I read each prayer the music came, not of my own will but from some deep well of inspiration that I didn't even know was there. The words and the music merged and became one thing, one expression of grace that I couldn't define, only live. When it was over I realized that an hour had barely passed, and yet all twelve prayers had been arranged to music. My life was different and I knew it. Some questions were answered and others raised, but

I suddenly knew the direction of my life, and that the peace prayers of the world would be its centerpiece.

What happened next has been covered in so many books and articles that it doesn't need to be mentioned here, only that an adventure began that continues to this day. The peace prayers that sang their melodies to me took me around the world, often to places where I would never have dreamed of going – Iraq, Northern Ireland, Kosovo, Serbia, East Timor, Israel, Bosnia and Croatia. Something was triggered in people when they heard the prayers, and I began to think that there was something to this idea of mass numbers of people getting together and joining their hearts in prayer. Maybe they were more than nice songs or beautiful prayers. What if music was the best way to get people focused on unity and compassion, and the peace prayers were just an excuse for us to realize the enormous power we have? Everything that had ever happened to me was suddenly falling into place, all the pious wanderings of my youth and my zeal for peace. Just as they tend to do now and then, the tumblers of my life suddenly fell into place.

Much of the current movement of my life began when in 1998 I received an official invitation from the government of Iraq to come to Baghdad to perform the Peace Concert in the same week that the US and Britain were preparing to launch the first bombing campaign since the Gulf War. I remember the fear I felt when I arrived in Amman, Jordan, and again when I began the twelve-hour taxi ride to get into Iraq. (The embargo made flying into the country impossible.) It wasn't the first time I had been called to join my brothers and sisters in a country at war, but there was something about this situation that made it unique, a feeling of urgency that defined the whole journey.

When I finally arrived in Baghdad I was taken to the El Rasheed Hotel, one of the most beautiful hotels in the Middle East, and as I gathered my things from the back of the taxi I noticed a beautiful but strange mosaic on the pavement by the entrance. The central figure on this mosaic was a man's face, a snarling face like a crazy person or an animal. The fact that one had to actually walk over this mosaic to enter the building was strange as well, and as I did so I thought I noticed something familiar about the face. It looked like George Bush, the American President who was in office when Iraq suffered the humiliating pounding in 1991. I stepped back to take a closer look. There below the mosaic were the words (in English): "Bush is a criminal." I realized with the suddenness of a cannon blast that I had arrived at my destination.

And yet my experience with the people of Iraq couldn't have been in greater contrast. They were not only polite and welcoming, but it was obvious that we all shared the same goal – to find a way out of the political chess-game without further destruction. Most people I met seemed to have a silent distaste for Saddam Hussein, but the fact that vocal dissent would certainly result in imprisonment or death kept the silence intact. I was taken to parties and did dozens of interviews. It was obvious that I was a kind of 'poster child,' an obvious attempt by the Iraqi's to look good in front of the rest of the world, but that didn't seem to matter at all. It was the final goal that was important, and we shared this single vision to the end.

I had asked my assistant to send an e-mail to a few people asking them to join me in prayer at the same moment that I would be performing the Peace Concert in Baghdad. I must admit that at the time I was a bit of an Internet virgin, and I had no idea that the announcement had circled the globe in about one week. When the moment came for the concert to begin, millions of people stopped what they were doing to pray peace in Iraq (later we'll go further into the significance of that statement, the difference between 'praying for peace,' and 'praying peace'). Three days later a peace agreement was signed, against the expectation of the whole world. At least for the moment, peace did prevail.

A week later I was invited to Stormont Castle in Belfast where the leaders of the warring political parties in Northern Ireland were locked in a battle of words and shrapnel. Though the country cried out for a peaceful resolution, it didn't seem to be anywhere in sight. Enter the power of 'praying peace' once again. As I sang the Prayer of St. Francis for the Northern Ireland Peace Conference, hundreds of thousands of people around the world stopped to pray, and once again a shift occurred three days later that allowed the agreement to be signed a month ahead of schedule. Though the basic issues that produce conflict have yet to be fully healed in Northern

Ireland, for a few short weeks humanity was able to sense the approaching tide of peace.

But more than anything I learned a very valuable lesson. For the first time in my life I saw the tangible results of mass prayer, not in a way that could be proven by statistical data, but in a way that many were nonetheless able to accept. It triggered a feeling of excitement in people, and the stage was set to take this experiment to the next level.

A month after the Iraqi and Northern Ireland peace vigils I met Gregg Braden and Doreen Virtue. It was the sort of meeting that takes place only a few times in one's life, when all parties feel the sacred shift that says: "Yes, this is important… pay attention and make the best of it." In one way or another our lives were pointing in the same direction, and the idea of using prayer to empower humanity was in the forefront of our imagination. The funny thing is that the idea for 'The Great Experiment' didn't even come from any one of us. It was a kind of joke at first, an idea that we heard from Steve Bhaerman, AKA, Swami Beyondananda. I don't really remember what the joke was, only that it made us all think a little more deeply. "Maybe he's onto something," one of us must have said. "Let's get science and mysticism together and try to prove that prayer is the most powerful force in the universe."

Weeks later, on April 23rd, 1998, millions of people in more than eighty countries joined us for the first ever 'Great Experiment'. Scientists had been contacted who promised to measure the effect of the vigil on the 'planet's heartbeat', a method of measuring the correlation between the planet's natural pulse and human consciousness that was very popular at the time. Though in the end, due to solar flare activity and a number of other factors, no firm data was gathered, one thing was clear – people wanted to come together and pray. And when they did, when mass numbers of people focused their minds and hearts on the reality of peace, things started to happen and prophecies were fulfilled.

For example, moments before 'The Great Experiment' began, I was at the United Nations in New York getting ready to speak to around forty ambassadors. Before they arrived someone suggested that the organizers and I should form a circle and say a prayer. When the prayer was over, a woman I didn't know stepped into the circle and said these words: "Four years, four months, four weeks and four days ago a group of native American elders came to the UN to give their vision of the New World. One of the things they said was, 'Four years, four months, four weeks and four days from now' (which is this very day), 'something will occur in this building that will shift the consciousness of humanity forever.'"

No one moved. "Can this be true?" I wondered to myself. None of us had heard this statement till that very moment, and yet, as I looked back, I remembered feeling very certain that April 23rd would be the day of change, and so it was. All I know is that I heard from literally thousands of people who said the same thing. They said that something happened to them that day, that they felt something shift not only within themselves but also in the whole world. Whatever it was, whatever those native elders had seen when they were themselves at the UN, millions experienced the power of a feeling based on mass prayer vigil, and nothing has been the same since.

My conviction that prayer is the most powerful force in the universe intensified, as did my relationship with Gregg and Doreen. The success of 'The Great Experiment' led to other worldwide prayer vigils, and each time that we invited people to come together as one mind and heart, something incredible took place.

For example, on November 13th, 1998, Gregg, Doreen and I were at a conference in Florida at the same time that another strike against Iraq seemed imminent. Once again, the word went out to the prayer community and thousands of people responded. We asked people to feel the reality of peace, and to know that peace is already present in Iraq. We were not praying for peace, but focusing on the peace that is there already, though buried beneath layers of confusion and distrust. Peace is the foundation of reality itself, we said, and when we focus on that reality, and then allow our spirits to come into resonance with that reality, then peace does indeed prevail on Earth.

The next morning Gregg entered the conference room with astounding news. Though we had no way of knowing this at the time, President Clinton had ordered an air strike against Iraq at nearly the same time that the prayer vigil was taking place. The jets were actually in the air waiting to begin launching their deadly weapons when something nearly unprecedented occurred. President Clinton gave two stand-down orders that night, and the jets returned to their ships without dropping a single bomb. At least for that night no one died, no one was injured, and we saw synchronistic evidence of a prayer vigil that changed the course of a world event.

And so, in the light of such stories each one of us needs to ask ourselves a simple question: "Are we willing to believe this evidence and allow for the possibility that there is a force in the universe that is more powerful and more reliable than any weapon ever made? Or will we choose to cling to our version of the Old World, the world where 'might makes right', and the best way to ensure a peaceful world is to have the biggest gun, the most powerful bomb, and the willingness to use them both?"

I, for one, believe the first. I can't prove beyond the shadow of a doubt that these vigils and the synchronous events were anything more than coincidences, or that the same outcomes would not have happened anyway. But I know in the deepest part of my being that there is only one law that rules all that we perceive, and that is the law of peace. Even when everything seems to contradict this law, when the insanity of humanity has escalated beyond the point of reason and control, still the reality of peace is evident, even in the places where it is most deeply hidden.

The goal of this book is to discuss the law that proves this point. In a way, this is a practical guide to peacemaking, though not from the usual perspective. Our goal is not to tell you how to make peace in the world, for that would imply that it is not already there. We aim to prove that peace is always present, and that it is the single law that defines who in truth we are. We could call it many things: love, compassion, grace, but for now we'll stay with the word that has defined my own journey to the Divine – Peace.

Yes, you do have the power to change the world, and you don't need to be famous or influential, or anything else that you might think is important. You just need to understand the law of prayer, and then apply that law. If you do, then everything will begin to change for you, first in your life, then in the world. Without even realizing it, you will be living the law that cannot be eclipsed by any power in this world. You will be 'Praying Peace.'

Chapter Two

In the summer of 1995 I had the chance to spend twelve amazing days in the mountains of Bosnia with a community of mystics who called themselves the Emissaries of Light. This book is not meant to go into the details of that journey, but needless to say what I learned when I was with them left an indelible mark on my consciousness and will forever influence the way I relate to the concept of peace. They said to me: "Our role is not to bring peace to where it is not, but to reveal peace where it is hidden." This one sentence became the foundation of my ministry, and as I began traveling to the areas of the world where peace was more than obscured by centuries of hatred and violence, I learned that they were not just words at all, but a powerful reality.

Peace, the Emissaries said, is not something that can be understood with the mind, but must be experienced with the heart. Try to grasp it and it is gone; try to write words to describe peace and it vanishes like the wind. And yet all of us, at one time or another, have felt this reality for ourselves and experienced its enticing aroma. It draws us in like a lover, not with words or grand gestures, but with the subtle movement of two hearts set afire by love's sudden approach. If we open our hearts and look with wide open eyes upon this ethereal presence, then it will appear in solid beauty before us, reminding us of all the ways it has claimed us in the past. Yes, even the hardest one among us has felt its rapture and has been overwhelmed by the fumes of its passionate wake. Even they cannot forget how they were overcome by the experience of peace.

But can words ever describe what we felt in those enlightened hours? Hardly. We can talk about a particular insight we learned or the lesson that seemed so obvious a week later, but our feelings... they are left for the lighter air that human lungs can never breathe. Peace is so much more than we can articulate, yet it is not more than we are, for if the experience of peace teaches us anything at all, it's that we come from the same source and are birthed in the same womb. Peace, then, is the essence of who we are, the very foundation of our lives. This is indeed the "peace that surpasseth understanding," for the more the mind tries to grasp its meaning, the more lost it becomes. But the moment it surrenders, forsaking the need to understand what cannot be defined, then it is clear, and nothing more needs to be said at all.

The Emissaries of Light said that peace is always present, that it is the simple truth of our existence. The question then becomes, "Where does violence come from? Surely good and evil exist side by side." The facts seem to prove this theory, for everywhere we look we see division, separation and the need for peace. How can peace be the foundation of a world such as this, where children starve to death everyday and ethnic wars rage for centuries? Isn't it our job to resist these evils and to actively fight against injustice? This, after all, is what we have always been told by all our heroes, all the men and women throughout the ages who have helped turn the tide of social discord.

Or did they? Certainly there is a legacy of social activism, those who have "fought the good fight" and resisted the disciples of violence and fear. Yet even among these people there are different modalities of action, and what works for one may not necessarily work for another. Martin Luther King promoted a non-violent revolution to ensure equality for all people regardless of their color or race, and Malcolm X shared his passion for peace. And yet these men did not always agree upon the appropriate method to bring about this end. King was a proponent of the Gandhi school of peacemaking, while Malcolm X confronted injustice with a different attitude. Same goal, different formulas.

Mother Teresa was once asked why she never participated in the anti-war demonstrations during the 1960's. She simply smiled and said, "I'll never go to an anti-war demonstration, but as soon as you have a pro-peace rally, I'll be there."

The Emissaries of Light are an example of a different school of peacemaking. They existed in the secret places of the world, like the mountains of Bosnia, working on the inner planes to bring about change on the outer. They never protested or raised their voices at all. They recognized that there is a deeper law where fundamental change is really made, and once this shift in consciousness occurs, then the outer world falls naturally into place. The question they asked is a simple one: "Is it better to work on the level of effect, or on the causal level where the effect is born?" This is really the essential question of this book.

So what does it mean to work for peace on the causal level? If their earlier statement is true, that peace is the foundation of reality itself, then it is toward this foundation that we must turn to find our answer. The Emissaries believed that reality is born in the mind and then extends into the world of form, not the other way around. Peace, then, can only prevail when the fearful patterns that allow conflict to exist are released, and this release must occur in the place where the conflict was born, which is the mind. How many times have we seen progress made in one area of the world or another through the use of what we'll call 'exterior peacemaking', only to be replaced by another level of discord? If you are tired of the furniture in a particular room of your house, what sense does it make to move the furniture around? It may look different, but the real problem has yet to be addressed.

From the Emissary perspective it makes more sense to remove the furniture and start over. If the chairs and sofas don't match the wallpaper, then find furniture that does.

But does this mean that we're to discard 'exterior peacemaking' altogether and sit in our rooms meditating all day? Not necessarily. The point the Emissaries made was that we cannot possess true wisdom until we address the problem where it really is, not where it seems to be. Then we will likely be inspired to act, but we will act from a new place, from a wider and more enlightened perspective.

Once again, Mother Teresa was a brilliant example of this. She did not run around the world with her fists clenched, filled with anger. She held the quiet space of compassion, and she extended that compassion to everyone she met. And when a particular situation required immediate action she did not hesitate for a moment but got off her knees to serve. And yet her smile never faded, especially when she held a dying man or woman in her arms. She was not fooled by what seemed to be happening, because her mind was so focused on what she knew was there. She saw holiness everywhere she looked, and that holiness became the foundation of her world.

Mother Teresa understood the difference between praying for something to happen, and 'Praying Peace.' Her life was a prayer, but it was not confined to the traditional definition of the word. She did not look upon a world that required peace, but on a world that was already healed. She didn't think that she was in Calcutta holding a dying child; she knew she was in Heaven holding the infant Jesus. And yet, her hands and her feet were in constant motion, for she realized that looking upon the 'real world' didn't mean denying someone's pain. "Give everything," she often said, "even when it hurts... especially when it hurts," but don't lose sight of the Vision of God that heals every ill and brings peace to every mind.

So what do the words 'Praying Peace' actually mean? Let's begin by defining a more traditional form of prayer, that of asking for something that we believe we do not already have. This is called a 'prayer of petition', which begins with perceiving a particular lack, and then believing that there is a God out there, sort of a spiritual Santa Claus, who can give it to us. There are a number of problems with this kind of prayer. Primarily it establishes and maintains a kind of spiritual dependency that we can never fully transcend. It is also the ultimate act of separation, the ego's need to be less than or separate from our Creator. The idea that we are One with God is seen as the greatest blasphemy, for we can never depart from the level of a servant, never enter into true communion with the Divine. To do so would really invite trouble, because then we would have to be responsible for what we create.

There is actually a technology of prayer that has been practiced for thousands of years, but which was lost to the West seventeen hundred years ago. I had suspected this for years, but it wasn't until my friendship with Gregg Braden deepened that I learned the actual details. In his book *Walking Between the*

Worlds Gregg focuses on the teachings of many ancient traditions and shows how these cultures possessed a very advanced understanding of the 'Science of Prayer', much more advanced than our so-called modern churches claim to possess. I began to appreciate this science on a whole new level, and Gregg's passion for the material began to rub off on me.

To the ancients, prayer was much more than asking for what they wanted. They knew that the mental decisions they made were only one part of a whole system that activates the creative power of prayer. The mind, they believed, is like a map. One can interpret the territory by reading the map, and can even determine the best route to take in order to arrive at a particular destination. But the mind cannot move the body to that destination. It needs help, like a car needs gas in it. Then the mind can work with the vehicle, directing its path, and so complete the journey.

In other words, a prayer that is centered only in the mind is a very weak prayer. It has no gas, and it is completely unable to move a person to the ultimate fulfillment of their dreams. Other elements are required, ingredients that when combined create an alchemical reaction. This is the basis of the science that mystics from every tradition have mastered and taught for centuries.

So what happened seventeen hundred years ago that made us lose this important technology? I personally don't believe it was a malicious decision that caused this information to be buried for so long. I like to think that it was due to ignorance, the belief that people weren't ready for such a powerful system.

In the fourth century the leaders of the Christian Church came together in Nice to determine an official doctrine that would be accepted by everyone. Some texts were adopted and others were rejected. The texts that conformed to the current version of Christian theology were bound together in a book that they ultimately called 'The Bible', and the others, dozens and dozens of rare manuscripts, were destroyed. If it had not been for the foresight of a few monasteries that buried these texts, we might never have realized what we had lost.

Soon after World War II, discoveries were made that rocked the world of Biblical scholars. In 1945 a peasant at Nag Hammadi in Upper Egypt uncovered a clay jar containing a library of thirteen papyrus books bound in leather, which are thought to have been buried by a Gnostic community. And then in 1947, among the mountains beside the Dead Sea in Israel, Bedouin nomads accidentally found a cave where quantities of holy texts had been hidden by members of the Jewish sect of the Essenes from the Qumran monastery nearby. They included the so-called Isaiah Scroll which is very different from the canonical Book of Isaiah. Many of the Dead Sea scrolls are fragmentary and, through ignorance of their value, some of the Nag Hammadi papyri were burnt. Nonetheless, for the first time since these books were marked for destruction, the modern world has regained a wealth of resources, and an insight into the mystical teachings of our ancestors. Many of these books were hidden from public view for decades, such was the transformative power of the contents. Only recently have most of them been released, and the contents have shocked the world. *The Gospel of Thomas* from Nag Hammadi, containing the sayings of Jesus, is still ruled heretical by the Vatican.

The wisdom of the Essenes, a mystical sect centered at Qumran, was far deeper and richer than most theologians had expected. It is now commonly accepted that Jesus himself was likely an Essene master, and many of his lessons and parables came directly from Essene teachings. But it is their contribution to prayer that we are concerned with here, and their contribution was vast.

This ancient community developed a system of prayer that was more reliable and scientific than anything we have today. It is possible that this wisdom was hidden from us because it was so powerful, and the goal of the early church was to establish the priests as intermediaries between Divinity and the people, something that would have been impossible if the people had been so empowered. And yet the real question here is not whether we were ready to harness this power seventeen hundred years ago. The question we should be asking ourselves is – are we ready now? Because now is the time that the information is finally made accessible to us.

To begin answering this question, let's look at the Essenes' fundamental teaching regarding prayer. The title of this book, *Praying Peace,* sums up the basic principle upon which every other principle of prayer is built. As Gregg Braden says, "We must become the peace we seek." In other words, the way to enhance any experience is to come into conscious resonance with that experience, or to vibrate at a similar frequency. In this sense the word 'Pray' means: to become, or to be like. If you want to experience peace, become peace. We are then able to experience ourselves as the source of prayer, rather than the beneficiary.

This idea is so foreign to our conventional understanding of prayer that you may be lost at this point. Think of it this way: When you pray 'for' something to happen, then you are focusing on the fact that it is not there already. This is the way most of us were taught to pray. The two main words the soul hears in this case are 'not there', and so this becomes the real prayer. The soul resonates with 'not-thereness', and therefore does nothing to attract the desired state.

But when we 'Pray Peace', what we are really doing is feeling as if the peace we seek is already there. We feel the completion of the prayer rather than the lack, and the soul responds accordingly. It begins to resonate with peace, drawing into its sphere the experience of peace, since this is what the mind has focused on. The prayer is answered automatically because the soul has followed an established code, attracting the state that has already been 'felt' rather than the experience that has been resisted.

As simple as this formula is, it has been the subject of suspicion and debate for nearly two thousand years. The idea that we are powerful spiritual beings has threatened the institutions that were meant to guard our Divine evolution. Why? Simply because the survival of an institution is sometimes more important than the truth upon which the institution was founded. Therefore, the truth must be hidden, unless we mature to the point that the institution loses power. After all, we often use religion in the same way that we use a business – to gain power and prestige. If people begin to realize that they are one with God and that no intermediary is required to experience our Divine Inheritance, then the institution will need to change its form, and this is the greatest threat for anyone who wants the institution to remain unchanged.

The ancients spoke about a time when all this would change, when the water would rise so high that the levy would finally break, flooding the whole valley with Light. Many people believe that we have now entered that prophesied era when peace prevails at last, and there are many signs that seem to affirm this theory. Most cultures have legends and stories about what will happen during the 'Great Shift', and these legends are being fulfilled at an alarming rate. And the release of these ancient texts corresponds with this as well, for how could it be a coincidence that sacred libraries buried for nearly two thousand years would be unearthed not more than two years apart?

Could it be that we are finally ready to realize our incredible power, and use it to create a world based upon the laws of love rather than the rules of fear? Has the time arrived when we begin to consciously implement the most powerful force in the universe?

And yet some of us may still find reasons for hanging back. It may happen that, as individuals, we are suspicious of our power. Perhaps we once unleashed it in a fit of anger, and seeing its devastating effects, have foresworn its use. We have been afraid that we lacked the purity to wield it without our imperfections creating unintended side effects. Will the experience of praying peace, of becoming peace, take us safely past this threshold so that suddenly, amazingly, we perceive ourselves as pure?

The purpose of this book is to examine and perhaps answer these questions. We're about to enter a kind of drama, like a performance that is meant to teach a particular lesson. Though Gregg, Doreen and I come from different backgrounds and disciplines, we seem to point toward the same goal. We each have something to say about how humanity can use prayer to create a world of peace, and though our approach may sometimes vary, the final end is always the same.

One day we got together and wrote out what we felt were the key elements of peace. After agreeing on what we called "The Seven Pathways to Peace," we sat down at a table and began the conversation that is recorded in this book. The subject was – How do we use these Pathways to realize and create a world of peace NOW? If this is the time we've been waiting for and if we are indeed ready for this time, then how do we take the step into the experience of peace? From the viewpoints of a scientist, a psychologist and a mystic, we endeavored to answer these questions, and to deepen our own understanding of the incredible opportunity that lies before us all. Though there are many other ways of looking at this subject, we offer these perspectives.

Relax because the curtain is about to go up and the play is about to begin. We hope you enjoy our little dramatization.

Section 2

The Seven Pathways to Peace

You are always praying; thought itself is prayer.

Whatever you focus your mind on, increases.

To change the world, change your thoughts about the world.

If you want to experience peace – become peace.

Peace is always present, though it is sometimes hidden.

Love is the only force in the universe.

The world is already healed.

Chapter Three

Now that we have laid the foundation upon which we will endeavor to enter the experience of prayer, it is time to begin our little play. "The Seven Pathways to Peace" is the only format that the actors will follow, otherwise the script is completely unrehearsed. We will begin by introducing the cast of characters.

THE SCIENTIST

The role of the Scientist is played by Gregg Braden, himself an earth scientist of great renown. He is the author of three bestselling books, the most recent being *The Isaiah Effect*, published by Random House.

THE PSYCHOLOGIST

The role of the Psychologist is being played by Dr. Doreen Virtue who is a practicing psychologist as well as the author of many books, including *Angel Therapy* and *Divine Guidance*.

THE MYSTIC

James Twyman, AKA the Peace Troubadour, is playing the role of the Mystic. He is the author of three other books, including *Emissary of Light* and *Portrait of the Master,* the latter published by Findhorn Press.

There are no elaborate sets, no dramatic overture, just three people sitting at a table with a single candle in its center and talking about the most powerful force in the universe – prayer. Each character speaks from the level of his or her own expertise, drawing from their experience examples and insights to support their convictions. In the end one thing will be clear – that though they approach the subject from different angles, every path does merge in the end, and every stream leads into the ocean of life.

Each scene begins with the narrator establishing the parameters for the evening's discussion. So sit back, open your mind and prepare to enter a New World, a world where every earthly power bows to the foundation of reality, the Mind of God that extends through each one of us at every moment.

The First Pathway

"You are always praying; thought itself is prayer."

NARRATOR:

To understand the Science of Prayer, we must first accept that our childish definitions of prayer can never encompass the true experience we seek. Many of us were raised to believe that prayer is something we do in church, or while kneeling at our bed at night reciting a laundry list like, "God bless this person or that person." As we grew older we learned to expand our appreciation to include those mystical moments when we were deep in meditation, lost in the higher realms where worldly thoughts can never ascend. The chants and mantras we learned were certainly stepping stones for the soul, but could they encompass the totality of 'Divine Communication' which is the ultimate goal of prayer?

What is this 'Divine Communication' meant to teach us? Would anything less than total union with God suffice, the experience that we are forever one with our Divine Source? And if this were so, then how can we separate one moment from another and say, "I am praying now, but I was not praying an instant ago." Is it possible to be thinking one moment but be completely void of thought the next? If the goal of any spiritual practice is the realization that we are one with God, then it stands to reason that every thought is shared. We cannot hide behind our private musings if communication with our Source has never been severed, except in our imagination. But what occurs in our imagination has no real effect. Therefore, our illusions have not kept us away from the truth, not even for an instant.

If this is true, then we are left with only one conclusion – that our prayers are not something we can turn on one moment and off the next, like a faucet that fills our glass only when we're thirsty. The fact is that we are always praying, and that every thought is a prayer in disguise. The flow of energy between our Creator and ourselves has not changed. And yet we have fallen into a dream that makes it seem as if we are separate and alone, convincing us that our thoughts are as solitary as our physical bodies. The key is not to confuse a dream with reality, and that's what the experience of prayer is meant to teach us.

And so, we enter a dialogue between three friends – a Mystic, a Scientist and a Psychologist. They come to the table each with their own unique vision, a different way of looking at the same reality, which is the experience of union and prayer. You may see yourself in one or in all of them. You may even hear your voice speaking through theirs. Whatever happens, sit down at the table next to them and listen for a while. It is time to discover what has never been lost, the source of prayer that has never been threatened by our silly dreams.

They sat down at the table and looked at one another. Then the conversation began:

"The First Pathway regards the way we think," said the Mystic. "We have been told that every thought is a prayer. The Pathway says: 'You are always praying; thought itself is prayer.' We're here to add our own thoughts to this sacred fire, our own prayers, then watch as the smoke rises to the Heavenly altar where our thoughts become the extension of the Mind of God. Who would like to begin?"

The Scientist leaned forward. The light of the candle danced in his eyes.

"In the tradition of the ancient Essenes, the mystical Jewish sect where much of our modern wisdom finds its root, a clear distinction was made between our thoughts, feelings and emotions. Though in our world they are very similar, to these masters there were subtle differences that made them unique. When they are bound together, they become the technology we call prayer. The Essenes said that our emotions are the force that drives us forward, but without a directional system our emotional energy becomes scattered. Thought, then, provides the direction we need while emotion provides the power, and when these two things merge then you have the 'feeling' world. So in other words, we may not separate our thoughts from our emotions, because from the Essene perspective it's the union of these two things that creates the feeling which is the real prayer."

"In psychology we would look at something we call 'selective attention,'" said the Psychologist, sitting back in her chair. "Our thoughts are indeed prayers, and yet we tend to focus only on those thoughts that we expect to be there, filtering out the ones we can't face, or don't want to face. In essence, we wear blinders that only let us see the things we want to see. Therefore, our world is filled with the images our thoughts have allowed, and the world we see is the subtotal of all those thoughts. Its only when we release those filters that we see our thoughts as they really are, as the prayers that create the world we perceive."

"Our thoughts are more powerful than we can ever know," the Mystic added. "If we are one with the Mind of God, then our thoughts are the prayers that create new worlds, banish old worlds, and imagine worlds that can never be. We have always created in this way, since the beginning of time, whether we want to realize it or not. The world we perceive is the world we want to perceive, just as you both said. We have made this world, and that's the same as saying that God made it because we are not separate from God. We often ask, 'How could God make a world where so much hatred and war exists?' And the answer is that we made the world ourselves, with God's full consent, not because God is without compassion, but because we need to realize just how powerful we are. What better way to do that than to look out at the world we despise, and realize that it is the result of our prayers."

"That can be frightening," the Psychologist said, "but sometimes that kind of scare wakes us up. From a spiritual psychological perspective, as *A Course in Miracles* says, 'It is impossible to have an experience you did not ask for.' Nothing happens by chance, and we need to realize that if we are to step into our true power. Everything in our lives is the result of prayer. It's not necessarily the result of being on our knees saying, 'Dear God, give me this or that.' Prayer can include worrying, obsessing, your goals and aspirations, and everything in between."

"Imagine how the world will look when we fully realize this power," the Scientist said. "Wars and conflict exist because we think we're weak, or because we don't understand how our feelings create the world we live in."

"Yes," agreed the Psychologist. She stood up from the table and began to pace around the room. "Wars exist because we're getting something we want from them. So the question is, what does conflict give us? Maybe it lets us live in a world where we don't have to be responsible. Maybe we're afraid of our own power. The idea that our thoughts are prayers seems to be very frightening to the person who wants to believe that we are separate from God."

51

Then the Mystic turned toward the Scientist and asked: "You said that prayer is not only a technology, but a science. What does that mean exactly?"

"When I say that prayer is a science, what I mean is that we can embark upon this path consistently, repeatedly and predictably, getting the same outcome each time. The technology is how we decide to apply this science. The fact is that we have been consciously using our thoughts, emotions and feelings as prayers for thousands of years, and their power has been proven over and over. This is not a modern concept we are proposing, but one that has been held by the ancients since time began."

"But what about when someone prays for something and it does not happen?" the Psychologist asked. "How can you say that we consistently achieve the same outcome?"

"This is the difference between praying with our thoughts alone, and praying with our thoughts and emotions combined," the Scientist replied. "When we ask people to 'Pray Peace', we're asking them to 'feel' the peace they seek, or to establish peace within themselves. When we do that then we set up a resonance pattern that attracts the thing we feel. When we follow the science of prayer then the same results are demonstrated over and over."

"It would be more true to say our emotions are prayers just as much as our thoughts," the Mystic said, "because it is the combination of these two things that creates the feeling that is heard by God."

"That's correct," the Scientist added. "Our feelings are the real language that our Creator responds to, much more than the words. If the words we say are divorced from our emotions, then the prayer has no real power. It sits upon the ground like a lead weight, never experiencing the fulfillment of the spoken desire. Likewise, emotions without thoughts have no real direction and never find the intended mark. But when we link these two experiences, bringing them together like a bow and arrow, then the prayer flies to the target with speed and accuracy. This is the way we link with the Mind of God, for God understands that creation is the result of both these elements working together."

"In the past, and even in the present, many people have thought that if they said the same affirmation over and over, it would change their lives," said the Psychologist. She was pacing to and fro beside the table. "But if their lives didn't change, they would give up the practice. What they had forgotten was to add the emotional element to the affirmation. If they did that, then they would enter into the feeling of the affirmation and it would easily be fulfilled."

"I believe this is how God creates," said the Mystic. "And this lesson teaches us to create like God by attuning our minds to the 'Technology of Prayer.' With your permission I would like to change the Pathway to read, 'Your feelings are prayers, and are the result of your thoughts and emotions.'"

"Your point is well taken," said the Psychologist, finally sitting down in her chair. "But it really doesn't matter what words we use, as long as we understand the truth ourselves."

And there, for the moment, the conversation ended.

The Second Pathway

"Whatever you focus your mind on, increases."

NARRATOR:

We now enter a new level in this unfolding, where we become aware of the awesome responsibility we have in manifesting the world we desire. In Act One we discovered how our thoughts and emotions congeal into the feelings that allow us to communicate with the Divine. Now we must learn how to become conscious of this active process, and in doing so we recognize that we are one with the creative power of the whole universe. This is when we discover the true meaning of prayer, and only through this realization does "the peace that surpasseth understanding" become clear.

We are learning the art of creation, discovering that we have within us the same power to create as God. In fact, this is all we have ever done – forge the world we have held in our minds and in our hearts. Our prayers have reached further than we expected, and now that we are aware of this power a whole new universe opens before us. We recognize that everything we perceive is the result of a prayer. It is easy to admit this about the things in our lives that we love, but what about those things we would rather replace? Are we able to say, "Yes, even these things were prayers born in my heart and extended through my feelings. I take responsibility for everything in my world."

This one line: "Everything you focus your mind on, increases," holds an important key to the mysteries of creation. Another way of saying this is: "Water only the seeds you want to grow, and don't water the ones you don't want." Every emotion, thought and feeling is a prayer, or a seed that is capable of growing into a mighty tree. Isn't that what Jesus meant when he said: "If you had faith no bigger even than a mustard seed..." He understood the laws of creation, and he realized that prayer was not something reserved for some moments and not for others. He was always praying because he was always feeling, and this, as we learned in Act One, is the real language that God cannot ignore.

And so we return to our table, to our actors, and continue our discussion on the power of prayer. We have only entered the door, for there are still so many important things to discuss, so many Pathways to grasp. Stand behind them and listen very close, and the answers will come to you, and you will begin to hear your own prayers like gentle whispers in the night.

"Let us continue now with the second Pathway," said the Mystic. "'What you focus your mind on, increases.' I feel as if we have entered a portal of some type, for this Pathway requires so much of us."

"It requires the one thing we have tried to avoid," declared the Psychologist, "...responsibility. There is something in the human psyche that wants someone else to be responsible for what happens to us... the world, God, etc. But rarely are we able to look in the mirror and see the truth, that there is only one face reflecting back at us, and we are responsible for everything we experience."

"It is the end of victimhood if we take this Pathway seriously", the Scientist added. "What can it mean but that we create everything we experience by focusing on it? Our attention is like a magnifying glass and everything it looks upon grows large and important."

"Yes, I agree with both of you," the Mystic said. "But I also expect that there is more, as if our vision does more than increase what we focus on, it actually creates it."

"Creates it in what way?" asked the Psychologist.

"Well, we have been toying with one idea that is hard to say outright, because the ego, and society itself, says we are wrong and would condemn us for such remarks. We like to say things like, 'We are one with God,' but what does that really mean? It obviously means that we are not separate from our Creator, but it would also mean that we create as God creates. This is the key to the Pathway... to all the Pathways."

"This goes back to the understanding the ancients had of the technology of prayer," the Scientist said. "It's not that our prayers are powerful, as if praying is something we do...it's something we are. We are powerful, and real prayer happens when we link our mind with the source of creation. We are the prayer, then. It is not separate from us, but it is what we are in truth."

"And so the question is, why don't we realize this power?" the Psychologist added. "And why have we created a world where sickness, pain and death seem to be real? According to this Pathway, these things have increased because we focused on them. I would venture to say that we used our prayers, or our emotions, thoughts and feelings, to create a world that would somehow prove we are guilty. There seems to be something in us that won't accept our holiness, therefore it focuses on guilt instead."

"And the world we perceive reflects that guilt," the Mystic said, finishing her thought. "Of course, that must be true if our original premise is accurate. That is why the Second Pathway is so important because it forces us to look upon the world exactly as it is and to be responsible for its effects. If we realize that our prayers link us with the creative power of the Divine, then we cannot create a world of peace until we take full responsibility for the world of fear."

"If we look at this from the perspective of the Isaiah scrolls and the Essenes in general," the Scientist said, "all possibilities that we can ever imagine are already in existence. We simply choose which of these realities we want to focus on."

"That adds an extra twist to our puzzle," the Psychologist told him. "It's not so much that the world we focus on increases, but that we pull the world we want into our attention through the decisions we make."

"That's correct," the Scientist continued. "The Essenes understood that there are an infinite number of universes existing at once, and now science is beginning to confirm that ancient belief. Scientists have been able to observe multiple universes in the same space in the laboratory. That means that the mystics have always been right, that the world is not the linear universe it seems to be, but a vast multidimensional universe with an infinite number of possible outcomes."

"So there is a world where peace has always been the rule," said the Mystic, "and yet we have chosen to look upon a different world. If there are, as you said, an infinite number of possible universes, all of which exist NOW, then why don't we choose one where conflict and war have been eradicated? It's simple really, though very unfortunate. We have decided we want war more than peace. And yet I believe that is changing now."

"The fact that we are able to have this discussion proves it is changing," said the Psychologist. "We are not separate from or more enlightened than the average person. The fact that we are able to consider these possibilities means that there are others who are considering them as well. And when enough people in the world realize the power of their prayers, and then focus on peace – then we will draw that world into our conscious attention. It begins with an individual decision, but then extends to encompass the collective consciousness."

"I believe that just now, after thousands of years, we are remembering the technology that allows this to occur," the Scientist said to them. "We have been so focused on the intellect that we didn't have all the ingredients in place to activate the science of prayer. It's only when we combine our thoughts and our emotions that a feeling is produced that has the power to determine the reality we experience. In other words, our outer world mirrors what we become within. As we choose a quality of thought, emotion and feeling, creation responds by bringing that to us, and in effect, answers our prayer."

"To focus our mind on something is essentially to make a decision about what we desire," the Psychologist said. "We sometimes call this goal setting. The angels say, 'Our intentions create our experience.' We are not victims of a world that is outside our control. Our intentions are prayers, just as you both said, and the thoughts to which we give energy determine what will come to us. That, I believe, is the essence of the Second Pathway."

"And yet all these truths come back to one single idea, expressed so eloquently in the First Pathway," the Mystic told them, as if beginning to wrap up Act Two. "'We are always praying,' every moment of every day, for we have within us the same power that created everything we perceive. Peace is achieved by realizing that power, then creating a world that is in alignment with the Will of God, not the ego. These Pathways are just a reminder, a way of suggesting what we have always known. But knowing it with the mind is not enough. We must know it through our emotions and feelings as well, and then will we be known by God."

The Third Pathway

*"To Change the World,
change your thoughts about the World."*

NARRATOR:

We have established that what we call the 'World' is intimately linked with our thoughts. They are not separate at all, but tied to one another like a balloon tied to a string. Our decisions about a particular event determine more of what we perceive than the actual happening. How many times have you been with a group of people who, you thought, all saw the same event? And yet, when you questioned them further, a different picture arose. One person saw one thing, and another person interpreted it in a completely different way. Everyone seemed to see the same physical event, yet their perceptions revealed totally different worlds.

Our prayers create the world we perceive, and we are always praying. This, at least, is what we are able to glean from the first two Pathways. But what do we do if we do not like the world our thoughts have produced? How do we claim the power of our emotions, thoughts and feelings and create the world we want, a world based upon the laws of love rather than the rules of fear? This is clearly the next step, the next level in the drama of our awakening. Can the World actually change with a simple shift in our consciousness, or is it how we've always been taught, that we have to beat it into changing?

This is the question the great minds of our planet have been battling with for thousands of years. Science has had its answer, psychology has given us a different slant, and spirituality has presented its own distinct point of view. What is unique about this time in history is that all these disciplines are beginning to say the same thing. If you imagine wisdom being like the spokes of a wheel, the closer we come to the center hub the more intimate we become with its truth. This being said, is it possible that we have come to a time where the truth itself has brought each of these perspectives very close together? And if this is so, that science, psychology and spirituality are realizing the same truth, could it really be a symbol that we are all moving together, and so realizing the power of our joined mind?

This is the reason why these three people have come together, to look at these issues, these Pathways, from different perspectives, with the clear expectation that they will meet at the same place. The truth, like a mountain, has many paths, some of which wind up its sides and others which shoot straight to the top. But just as there is only one truth expressed in a multitude of ways, so do we find ourselves together even when we seem furthest apart.

"We now take under consideration the Third Pathway," the Mystic said to the others. "It says, 'To change the world, change your thoughts about the world.' Who would like to begin?"

"I have something I would like to add," the Psychologist said. "We have heard these same words expressed in many ways, that each one of us has the power to change the world. I would like to point out two different ways of looking at this idea. There are actually two different worlds we're referring to. The first is the world of the individual mind, and the second is the collective world. It is easy to see that the collective world is made up of billions of little universes, all held within the mind of every person on the planet. The question is, how do all these seemingly separate versions of the world combine to create an experience we can agree upon?"

"Better yet," the Mystic added, "if the collective world is really just the manifestation of smaller worlds, is there any reality in either one? In other words, are the physical laws that we perceive subject to real forces, or just to the emotions, thoughts and feelings we agree upon? Maybe they have no 'reality' at all outside the force of our prayers."

"From a scientific perspective both would be true," the Scientist said to them. "There really isn't a difference between the two. Our emotions, thoughts and feelings draw upon the raw materials we are given, like the resources of a planet for example, and use them like building blocks to create what we're calling the 'world.'"

"Yes, but where do those raw materials come from?" the Mystic asked him. "We normally begin with the premise that we either evolved or landed here, looked around at the stones and wood and began building a logical world. I sense that there is something deeper happening though, that we were more responsible than we think. What if none of this happened to us, but by us?"

"It sounds like your suggesting that we created the planet," the Psychologist said.

"I'm not suggesting it as much as I'm asking the question. We keep talking about how powerful we are, and we say that we are one with God. We sometimes say that God created the world, everything we perceive here on this planet of ours. So, if we're one with the Mind of God, then we were not isolated from that genesis. Whether we were conscious of it or not, if God has existed forever then we have existed forever as well, in one way or another. Maybe not in the way we perceive ourselves now, but real nonetheless. The whole tree rests in the silent memory of the seed. Right? If this is true, then the original 'stuff' of creation is within us, just as everything is within us. We were present, then, when these 'raw materials' came into being. We have been present through it all."

"This is very much like the hologram analogy," the Scientist said. "The whole is contained within each part. If you break a hologram into a thousand pieces, nothing has really been lost because the original pattern is still intact."

The Mystic jumped up from the table. "Exactly!" he said. "That's exactly what I'm saying. We, each one of us, contain the whole pattern. We, in the largest sense imaginable, created the world through the language of the soul, and we can change it in the same way."

"And that is what the Pathway means," the Psychologist said. "If we change our thoughts about the world, then the world must change, because the thoughts of God, of which we are forever part, created everything that exists."

"The key is to let go of the ideas we have about what we are and what we are not," the Mystic continued. "To say that we are one with God, or that we have within us the 'stuff of God' is just another thought until we enter into the experience of this truth. In other words, just as the Scientist has been saying, a thought is not very powerful when it is divorced from the emotion, but when the thought and emotion combine they produce the feeling, and this is where creation begins. We're not here to accumulate more ideas or intellectual thoughts, but to actually experience the truth. We have convinced ourselves that such an experience is impossible, but I believe we've come to a point in our spiritual maturation where it is not only possible, but required."

"What the ancients are saying to us in the words of their day," said the Scientist, "And what we're now rediscovering through the modern language we call science, is that our

66

outer world mirrors what we have become from within. As we choose peace, compassion, understanding and forgiveness, these are mirrored back to us in our outer world as global peace, gentle weather patterns, and cooperation between governments and nations. As we choose anger, hate, jealousy and revenge, it comes back to us as unsettled weather patterns and the conflicts we see between governments and nations."

"So you're saying that the world responds to our thoughts in a direct manner," said the Psychologist. "Science has more than suspected there is a connection between thought and the larger world, it has admitted to it."

"Science has laid the foundation for this," continued the Scientist. "Yes, this is a very common premise now. Science has shown a statistically measurable relationship between populations and high or low-pressure weather systems, and even earthquake centers. They can't say it is definite, but they do say that there is a high correlation between where large populations are in a state of unrest and where these weather patterns are forming, and even where the earth changes are taking place."

The Psychologist shifted in her chair, then looked at her two friends saying: "From a psychological perspective, more and more people have stopped looking to politicians or other authorities to change the world. It keeps coming back to the individual being responsible for the whole world. If we all behaved self-responsibly, took care of our own self in order to manifest what makes us truly happy, then the world would change to reflect those decisions. So once again, it's an inside out job, not outside in."

"I would like to go back to what the Scientist was saying about weather patterns and earthquakes," the Mystic said as he sat down again at the table. "There have been so many predictions, both scientific and psychic, of earth changes that never happened. Would you say that it's because we changed our minds about them?"

"That's exactly what I would say. We decided to go through these shifts in a gentle way, and the earth responded accordingly. In California, for example, the earth's crust is responding with very long, continuous tremors rather than with violent ones. It began several years ago but never causes much damage, it's so slight that most people don't even feel it. To science these are anomalous indicators, but to the ancients this was part of the relationship between our thoughts and the Earth itself. We are tuned to our world, and what we feel or become our world mirrors back to us. By the same token, when we see patterns of disorder, in our oceans and rainforests for example, that's also mirrored in our bodies as the conditions and diseases that prevent us from expressing life."

"Everything we are saying leads to one conclusion," said the Mystic. "Everything is joined as one. There is only one Mind expressing itself in an infinite number of ways, as people, as nature, as planets...all from a single source that we call God. Separation is an illusion, and this is being proven and accepted by each of us in our specific areas of expertise."

The Fourth Pathway

*"If you want to experience Peace,
Become Peace."*

NARRATOR:

How does one become peace? Better still – how do we live our lives in such a manner that everything we do is an expression of compassion, kindness and love, where we become a walking, breathing 'Prayer of Peace'? St. Paul implored the early Christians to "Pray without ceasing." Isn't this what we've been doing? If we have come to realize anything through this conversation, it's that all our thoughts, feelings and emotions are prayers, and that it is impossible for us not to pray without ceasing. The real question becomes, "How do we 'Pray Peace' without ceasing, focusing all our energy on this one goal so that we actually become that which we seem to be seeking?"

You have within you the same power that created the whole universe. Are you willing to accept this fact? Are the words, "I am one with God," true or is it just a concept that gives us a moment's pause, a pat on the back before we bee-line back to our old way of thinking? And what are these old thoughts that we have clung to so desperately? How about: "My soul is one with God, but the rest of me isn't," or "I may be one with God, but if God knew what I have done..." Do these thoughts ring a bell? Do they sound familiar at all, touching a deep place within your heart that is still afraid of love, still afraid to look at the truth in you?

We all have those dark corners in our mind, those shadowy figures that rise to threaten our awakening. That's what being on this planet is all about. That's why we're here, to heal a single thought, a simple idea that has ruled nearly every aspect of our lives, demanding our full attention: "I am not worthy of love." That's it. What if we're wrong? (Are you willing to accept that possibility?) What if God never saw your so-called indiscretion, whatever it is you think you did that is so bad, so unforgivable. What if you were forgiven the instant the idea flashed into your mind? That would mean that all the guilt we feel is unnecessary, that it serves no real function. Wouldn't that be a wonderful, life-altering realization?

Forgiveness is the key, the path that leads away from guilt and into the Light. You will see in a moment, in the course of our conversation, that this is where all paths lead in the end, the final resting-place of sin, sickness, pain and even death. Look to the heart of any discipline, any worldly path or endeavor, and you will find this one formidable truth. Healing cannot happen till we let go of the past, till we allow old blocked energies to dissipate, creating space for a new life to be born. Forgiveness is the only way

71

we can release the shadows that have halted our own spiritual ascent, for in the end, who is there to forgive but ourselves?

How do we become peace? It's very simple really – by realizing that the peace we seek is the very foundation of our existence. It is what we are, the truth in us. We cannot become something we already are, but we can remember what we have forgotten. That is the key. We have piled layer after layer of false beliefs atop that truth, and have decided to focus our attention on a shadow. Forgiveness, then, is the willingness to let all those shadows go and to remember the gift our Creator gave us when we came into being – Life. Life knows only life, and gives but unto life. This is not a puzzle to wrap your mind around, but a simple reality we need to recognize. Are you willing?

Once again the Mystic looked at the piece of paper lying in front of him on the table and read the Pathway written upon it.

"The Fourth Pathway says: 'If you want to experience peace – Become peace.' I think that I'll begin our discussion this time. This is a very profound statement, one that we have all touched on in one way or another. We spoke earlier about the law of resonance, the fact that similar frequency patterns tend to be drawn to each other. In other words, we draw into our lives the experiences and people that correspond with our image of ourselves. If we believe we are good and trustworthy, then we'll tend to attract people who are the same. But if we hold a darker image of ourselves, then we are likely to bring people into our lives that reinforce that image, reflecting what we believe to be true about ourselves.

"If the theory of resonance is true, then it should easy for us to determine the best way to become emissaries of peace. We cannot bring something to another unless we believe we have that thing within us, or that state of being. To bring peace, we must find that place within us that is peace. It's that simple."

"But what if a person has no experience of that state?" the Scientist asked. "What if their life has been anything but peaceful?"

"That's a good question, and one that any reasonable person should ask. The answer is very important as well. I think we can all agree that there are ultimately only two emotions we are capable of, and that every other emotion we experience is a derivative of one or the other. The first emotion or experience is love and the second is fear. We have also said, all of us in our own way, that there is only one force in the universe, and that this force is what some of us call God, or maybe the 'Single Unified Consciousness.' God, at least my concept of God, is all-loving. That would mean that only love exists, since it is the product of a Divine Mind that is all pervasive. What is fear then? Is it possible that it is nothing more than a shadow, or perhaps the denial of the experience of love? And is a shadow a 'real thing,' possessing real power or real effects? I would say no, for it is not the opposite of love, but rather the obstruction of love. What is all pervasive can have no opposite."

"That all sounds true," said the Psychologist, turning to face the Mystic. "But how does it apply to today's Pathway?"

"It's simple, really. If love is the foundation of reality, then that means it's active, real and present no matter what, even when it doesn't seem to be. A moment ago the Scientist asked how someone who has never known peace could experience it. Peace, quite obviously, is a derivative of love, not fear. It's within us, even within the person who seems most isolated from the experience, because they cannot be separated from what knows no boundary. Perhaps the peace is hidden beneath many layers of fear and mistrust, but it is there nonetheless. Otherwise God would not be all-loving. Otherwise God would have an opposite. I firmly believe that God has no opposite, therefore love is always present, always the foundation of our being, even when fear seems to have eclipsed its radiance."

"I see where you're going," said the Psychologist. "If only love exists, then peace is always present even when it is not apparent. And the law of resonance, which corresponds to the Second Pathway, states that if we focus on a particular experience, even if it is buried, then it must increase."

"Exactly," rejoined the Mystic. "So, even if a person has very little experience of peace, if they focus on love then they must experience love. This is how we become peace, then, simply by focusing on it.'"

"The ancients didn't have the language of science which we have today," said the Scientist, "so in their language they said that we have forgotten how to love ourselves. Their remedy was what they called the 'Eleventh Commandment.' It invites us to love our Creator with our whole heart, our whole mind and our whole soul."

"That is the same thing that Jesus said," the Psychologist added.

"That's because Jesus was an Essene, and the concepts he used to teach truth were Essene concepts. They were asking us to merge our thoughts, feelings and emotions because they knew that that was how we 'become' our prayers. Also, when these three things merge and become one, that's when we have the power we call love. Jesus and the Essenes asked us to love God completely, with all our energy. And there is a very important reason for that. They knew that when we love our Creator, we are actually loving ourselves because we are one with our Creator. And the opposite is true as well – when we love ourselves, or anyone else, then we are in truth loving God."

"Your science is drawing very close to my mysticism," the Mystic said.

"Of course it is," the Scientist continued. "That's because truth knows no boundaries. The truth is true, whether expressed through the language of science, psychology or mysticism."

"But we need some way for people to access this truth," the Psychologist said. "Otherwise these are just high ideas and concepts that cannot be applied. I would suggest, at least from a psychological perspective, that the best way to apply everything we are expressing here today is through forgiveness."

"Once again, we are aligned," the Mystic said to her. "The same would be true from a spiritual point of view as well. But I would suggest a level of forgiveness that is very different from what most people are accustomed to. Forgiveness is normally understood as something we offer to someone who has offended us in some way. This is not forgiveness at all, it is an attack. It is really saying, 'You committed an offence against me, and I, in my greater wisdom, am willing to forgive you.' All this does is create separation and continue the conflict."

"From your perspective," the Scientist asked, "how would you define forgiveness?"

"We are being asked to forgive as God forgives. We are asked to look past the offence altogether, not judging if someone is worthy of our mercy, but bestowing it equally upon all."

"I would agree with that," the Psychologist said. "The forgiveness you are speaking of brings people closer together because it does not demand retribution. I often ask people to make a list of everyone they can think of who has offended them in any way, then release each person in love. This is very similar to the theory of resonance, which the Mystic spoke about earlier. When we look past the offence that seems to have occurred, then choose to focus on the love that is the foundation of our true relationship, then the experience of love increases. We become that love then, because we were willing to give it to another."

"So, to sum up what we are all saying," the Scientist said, "we become that on which we focus our thoughts, feelings and emotions. And yet, since love is the foundation of reality, it is the only experience that extends forever because it is synonymous with the Mind of God. Anything that is not aligned with this force is not real, but only a shadow of reality. Do you both agree with this assessment?"

They both nodded their heads, and the discussion, at least for that moment, ended.

The Fifth Pathway

"Peace is always present,
Though it is sometimes hidden."

Narrator:

This book, this drama, has only one real lesson it seeks to express: 'Only Peace is real'. In the last scene an important statement was made, one that will have continuing relevance as we continue along this path. Our characters agreed that there are only two experiences of which we are capable, and that every other experience is a derivative of one or the other. The first is love and the second is fear. Fear, it was said, is the shadow of love, and is therefore not real. We can make it seem real; we can make it feel real, but that doesn't make it real.

Let's spend some time, then, looking at the difference between 'reality' and 'seeming reality.' It would be easy for someone to look out at the world and decide upon the reality of fear, hatred and violence. Just look at modern society and you'll discover countless examples of how fear is not only present, but dominant. There is more drug abuse, domestic violence and war than ever before. How can we say it isn't real? Isn't that like an ostrich putting its head in the ground and pretending there's nothing to fear?

Certainly evil appears very real in this world. It would be irresponsible to deny the suffering of the people who are experiencing these assaults, or to be overzealous in our insistence that there are no true victims in the world. What we are examining now is a deeper motivation, one that is so ancient yet intimately present that we often take it for granted. Our goal is not to deny pain, but to offer the ultimate escape from it.

Most of us were raised to believe in what is called 'free will', the ability and right to make our own decisions and to create a world of our own making. Few of us have considered the possibility that the world we experience may be very different from reality itself. For example, when we dream, we have the ability to build a world that doesn't necessarily respond to the same laws we experience when we are awake. We can fly in our dreams, but not when our physical eyes are wide open. And yet, when we're in the 'dream world', we rarely consider this discrepancy. It feels very normal to fly, and so we do. It is not until we wake up that the 'new reality' imposes a new set of laws.

Is it possible that there is a deeper law that operates on a level which is unfamiliar to us in the ego world of bodies and personalities? What we call the 'world' is based on the law of duality and separation. We seem to be distinct individuals with the power to change our lives without necessarily changing the lives of those around us. We never consider that perhaps there is another world where duality is eclipsed, where love and fear are not seen as opposing forces. Could there be a universe just behind the veil of this one where love is the single law and fear is forgotten completely?

The Fifth Pathway states that "Peace is always present, though it is sometimes hidden." Behind the veil of our fear there is a vital energy that waits silently upon our attention. We can call this experience peace, or love, or a number of other things, all of which express our longing for a state beyond the dualistic universe. Where did this longing come from? Is it possible that there is a part of us that remembers an ancient reality, and we have been trying to get back to it ever since? It is hidden from our attention, yes, sleeping beneath countless layers of separating emotions. If it really is there, if this is something more than a concept we use to escape from the mundane world, then how do we access it?

The question you need to ask yourself is a simple one. Are you willing to consider these possibilities, or is it easier to toss them in the pile called 'too far-out to look at'. It will be hard for you to sit on the fence with this one, since the premise of this book is so opposed to everything we have ever been taught. Either society is right and this is all nonsense, or you have been wrong about everything. And if you have been wrong, what does that mean? Is it a sign of defeat, or the first glimpse of victory? Better yet – is there any difference between the two?

The three sat at the table and looked around at one another. The difference between the various disciplines and perspectives was becoming less and less obvious, as if they were now speaking with one voice, coming from a single reference point. Even the words were the same, and it was getting hard to tell who was the Scientist, who was the Psychologist and who was the Mystic. There were only three Pathways remaining, three subtle distinctions that outlined the metaphysics of peace. As always, the Mystic began by reading the Pathway out loud.

"The Fifth Pathways is: 'Peace is always present, though it is sometimes hidden.' Who would like to begin?"

The Scientist leaned forward and said, "Twentieth Century science suggests that all possibilities are already in existence, dormant until we awaken them through our thoughts, feeling and emotions. From that perspective, everything from the fiercest wars to our greatest social challenges, even the heights of ecstasy and peace, are already present and asleep within us. They wait upon our call to bring them into the world through the choices we make in each moment of our lives."

"Are you saying," the Mystic asked, "that every choice has already been made and that we pull the world we want into existence through our prayers?"

"Basically, yes," the Scientist continued. "Science has now proven that multiple worlds can exist in the same space at the same time. This is completely contrary to our former notions of how the universe works, and it shows how little we have known. Even now, with all our scientific advances, we have but a tiny glimpse of these things, but these glimpses show us two things. First of all, that it is impossible for our rational, intellectual mind to fully grasp the inner workings of the universe. The second is that there is obviously a part of us, though for most of us it is not conscious, that does understand and fully participates in the creation of worlds. We have always done it, and always will do it. What is happening, where all these disciplines come together, is that we're learning to be aware of what we have always done. When this occurs, then we will build not so much from our unconscious fears, but from our conscious experience of love."

"I agree," said the Psychologist. "This is the place where we all come together, all the ways we have of looking at the world. Since God is omnipresent, and since the only thing that is real is God and God's creation, then only peace is real. It's all there, we just haven't recognized it because we have been preoccupied with our fear, and have used a fearful mind to create. We have been praying fear, in essence."

"Yes, praying fear is exactly what we have done," the Mystic added. "And since the universe responds to what we ask it to respond to, fear has been the result of our prayers. We could have a different discussion about why we decided to do that, but for now we'll settle for the fact that we have. 'Why' doesn't matter at this point."

"The angels say that we're afraid of love," said the Psychologist. "We're so afraid of being hurt that we guard against love's presence, because it means we must take a risk. If we would release our past grievances against our parents, our lovers, our brothers and our sisters, then we wouldn't be so guarded against being hurt again. We would open our hearts to love."

"So how does all this apply to the Pathway?" asked the Mystic.

"We have said the same words in many different ways," the Scientist said. "Peace is real and present regardless of what we choose to be conscious of. If we deny what is real, then we live in a dream and we pull all the components that relate to that dream into our awareness. But that doesn't change the truth. Peace is still present. It is still real. The only thing that must change is our awareness."

"And this occurs when we stop being afraid of love," the Psychologist added. "This is really our only problem, being afraid of what is real, and choosing to experience what is just an illusion. What will happen when we realize this and accept what has always been true? I believe we are very near that day."

The Sixth Pathway

"Love is the only force in the universe."

NARRATOR:

Let's begin by examining the word 'force', and how it relates to the experience of love. Force is sometimes understood as a power that is exerted upon an object in order to move it from one position to another. Film lovers may recognize it as the energy that permeates all living beings, a definition made famous, of course, by "Star Wars." In this sense "The Force" also has a dark, sinister side which can be used to acquire and maintain power.

But how is love used as a force – the only force in the universe? This is clearly a continuation of the last Pathway, which stated that peace is always present. These statements, whether experienced as true or not, build upon one another like blocks that ultimately reveal a whole structure. They all, in one way or another, reveal the same truth, though from a slightly different angle or perspective. In this case, however, the truth the Pathway is meant to reveal is not at all clouded or disguised. It says what it means – "Love is the only force in the universe," and does not apologize for being blunt and direct. It demands attention, for you will either accept or reject its assertion, but you will not be able to ignore it.

The world we have perceived up till now says that two independent forces operate and must oppose one another – good and evil. The secular and religious alike agree upon this idea. There are those who do good in the world and those who do the opposite of good. There is God and then there is Satan. God has the choir of angels and Satan has the band of demons. All of these images reveal the polarity of the ego, which is the foundation of everything we believe in. To reject this idea, that good and evil can exist side by side, is to reject the world itself. And if we reject the world, what are we left with?

This is the basic question which this book seeks to answer. It questions this foundation and asks a new question: "What if there is only one force operating in the world – Love, otherwise known as Peace?" If this is true, then everything we have ever learned about the world and ourselves is meaningless. If we turn toward love then we are at peace, but if we reject it then we experience the shadow we call fear.

We have been taught to respond to everything in a certain way, to protect ourselves from any outside force that might potentially do us harm. But what if there is nothing on the outside at all but a world that responds to our thoughts, and shows us exactly what we expect to be in it. That would mean that we can change the world simply by changing our thoughts about the world. The world we have experienced till now has responded to the thought of 'two forces'. What would happen if we accept this Pathway? What if there is actually only one force?

This is the metaphysics of peace. The Pathways reveal a different world than the one we are accustomed to, one where peace is not created but where peace is the only thing that exists in reality. Accept this, and the world will change to reveal your new belief. Resist it, and nothing will change at all. We have more power than we can imagine – that statement has been made over and over in this book in many different ways. If we believe we are weak, then the world will continue to 'happen to us'. But when we realize who we really are, that we are one with the creative force that made everything, then the world 'happens by us', and we are able to bring peace simply by admitting we were wrong about war. What would such a change cost us? Are we willing to give up the world of two forces and accept the world of one?

If our drama reveals anything, it's that this truth is being expressed by many different disciplines, in this case by the scientific, psychological and spiritual. Perhaps for the first time in history we are able to examine the world from a new perspective, free of the restraints of past prejudices. What do we find? Quite simply, that most of our assumptions about the universe were wrong, and we need to reconsider everything, especially ourselves. Will we remain victims of the world we perceive, or stand up and accept the power that has been given to us from the beginning of time? One way or another we are going to have to take a long hard look at these things. Why not now?

When we left our characters they had come to an important realization. Though they seem to discuss each Pathway from different perspectives, in the end they are essentially saying the same thing. Take away the jargon and labels and you are left with one truth, one experience of the only force that exists in truth. That they agree to this premise is not a surprise, but the fact that their words are beginning to merge one into the other may be.

The Mystic looked at his friends and said: "We've come a great distance along these Pathways, and yet we've gone nowhere at all. We end where we began, in the realization that there is something happening in the world that is unprecedented. All our disciplines are revealing the same thing – that the world we thought we understood so well is a mystery to us, and yet it is clearly revealed to the truth of our souls. To the soul it is no mystery at all. We are always praying and creating the world we want to perceive. If we want to change that world, we need only change our mind about the world, for our thoughts, feeling and emotions are the source of everything we perceive. But we cannot experience that transformed world until we become that reality which we seek. If we want peace, then we must become peace. All these truths lead us to today's Pathway, the culmination of them all. 'Love is the only force in the universe.'"

"We have said this in so many ways already," the Psychologist said. "Love is beyond verbal description. Words can never come close to describing what love or peace is. Only the experience demonstrates the reality. Some people have to go through very dramatic experiences to get to that place – near death experiences or seemingly terminal illnesses. Only then do they begin to appreciate life, and focus all their energy on peace."

"From a scientific perspective," the Scientist said, "everything is joined in the end. That's probably as close as they can come to discussing love. They speak of unified fields or resonance patterns and admit that in these the forces extend further than we can ever comprehend. We could say that love is the only reality, and science would not disagree with that theory. It would only use different words to express it."

"Only God exists," the Mystic said. "All the ancient spiritual traditions have said this, in one way or another, while some still contend with another force called evil. I believe that one or the other is true. If we believe that only love exists, then evil cannot oppose love, except in our imagination. But what is held in our imagination cannot have real effect. It is limited to the world of dreams, while reality exists completely independently."

"The closest we can come to understanding this experience is by being in a state of gratitude," the Psychologist added. "That's the closest we can come to Divine Love, for it teaches us on levels we cannot understand with the intellect. If we all develop the habit of counting our blessings, even though it seems so basic or old-fashioned, then we would be so grateful for our life that we would actually attract love. That, after all, is what we're all looking for, because at a core level we all understand the truth in this Pathway."

"In the last seventeen hundred years," the Scientist said, "we have been invited to follow a path that says there is love, and then that there is the opposite of love, the light and the dark. As we view the world through that polarity, we see the same polarity in all situations, in all relations, and in our relationship with the Creator as well. The Essenes were very clear that at the deepest level of our esoteric traditions, love and hate are really one force, different only in the way we humans make it appear. In other words, there is a single force at work coming from a single Source or Creator. And it is that force we're invited to embody in each moment in our lives. We call that force love."

"That is a truly amazing way to look at this Pathway," the Mystic said. "Love and fear are really the same energy expressed in different ways. When we realize that, then we can allow them to move toward one another, two sides of the same coin in a way. We run away from fear and towards love, and sometimes we do the opposite. What if we remained perfectly still and let the single energy of truth extend toward us? Better still, what if we realized that that one energy extends from us continuously, and that we can never be separated from it except in our dreams?"

"This is another place where science, psychology and spirituality merge," the Psychologist said. "Energy is energy and it doesn't need to opposed. When we flow with whatever is happening, then we are able to see the love in every situation."

"Then we realize the truth of this Pathway," the Scientist said. "Love is the only true force in the universe, and anything that seems to oppose love is not real. Once again we come to common ground. We may as well throw away the labels and accept that we're saying the same thing."

"And so we are," agreed the Mystic. "In fact, there is becoming less and less to say at all. Everything is fading into an ocean of peace. That, I believe, is why we began this discussion in the first place."

The Seventh Pathway

"The World is already healed."

NARRATOR:

You have reached the point of no return. What will you do now? There are only two choices. The first is to fall back into the old familiar world where your dreams are not threatened by the strange ideas you have read in this book. The second is far more risky, and adventurous. Are you prepared to say "YES" to everything you have heard, all the evidence we have examined together? Will you go out on a limb and risk everything in favor of a world that is not chained to old beliefs, to all the ways you have limited yourself, the world, and even God? Are you ready to step out of the box?

The fact that you have stayed with us till now says something important. You could have turned back at any time, thrown in the towel and said, "No more of this!" Even if you thought this at one point or another, still you are reading, listening, waiting. You may not know what you're waiting for, but there is a part of you that heard the call and believes, as if the ancient memory is still there within you, longing to be released again. "Could it be true?" you may be asking. "Is all this even remotely possible?"

"The world is already healed." For the world the ego made, no statement could be more challenging. It is a direct assault upon everything the ego created, everything it holds dear. It goes contrary to all the evidence you have gathered around yourself, all the terrible images you hold in your mind to justify attack, defense and all the armaments that have protected you from what you do not understand. "The world certainly is not healed," you may insist. "Just look around yourself. If this is what healing is, then..."

Stop there. Lay aside this 'evidence' and consider something for a moment. What if you can change it all, you and everyone who thinks like you, just by making a new decision. What if the world has been this way because that's the way we wanted it to be, the way we asked it to be, for whatever reason? What if it helped justify an image we have held of a weak species that is at the mercy of nature, coarse motivations, and whatever other assurances we need to maintain such a world? And what if we have the ability to change all that in an instant, just by choosing love over fear? Don't be too quick to say it can't be so simple, because maybe it is. Maybe it was always up to us.

"The world is already healed." Breathe those words in for a moment. Consider that this statement is the very essence of truth, and that you have permission to enter that truth right now. Are you willing? Is it worth the risk, or is it easier to hold on to the status

quo, all the old patterns that have satisfied your need to be anonymous, secluded and alone? What would you lose, anyway? Is it hard for you to give up defeat? Is it impossible to accept that you have everything you need to be happy and content, no matter how things appear? If the world is already healed, then why should you be kept from it? Why should you live in despair when victory is so nearly yours?

These are all the questions we have been unwilling to ask till now. Maybe it's because we didn't know how to ask them, or didn't know that an alternative even existed. But you know now, and you can never go back again. You can close this book and retreat to the world that once seemed to make sense, but there will always be a part of your mind that will wonder if it was true. "What if..." you may ask yourself, and the answer will be the same. You cannot run from yourself, no matter how hard you try.

"The world is already healed." Seize it now. Grab hold of reality and don't let go, no matter how viciously your mind reels and spins. You have come too far to turn back now. There is too much at stake now that you have pulled aside the Wizard's curtain and seen the truth. You always had the power to go home, you just didn't realize it. But you can now, if you want to. You can open your heart and accept just how much God loves you, not the image you have made of yourself, but the truth in you. It really is not hard at all. It just hurts for an instant, but then the Light breaks through.

The three friends took a deep breath for they knew they were near the end of their discussion. The insights they had shared and the lessons they had learned from one another were nothing compared to the sudden bond they felt. Though they had sat down at the table as three individuals from three different schools of thought, they realized that they weren't as far apart as they had first thought. That, after all, was the real lesson of the Pathways, and they had allowed the current below the surface to pull them to the truth.

"We have come to the final Pathway," the Mystic said, "and it is a strange place for us to end. It is really a beginning, the realization of the real meaning of peace and the release of the world of despair. All the other Pathways flow into and away from this one. It says: 'The world is already healed.' Who would like to begin?"

They looked at one another as if it was wrong to intrude upon the silence of the moment. What was there to say that hadn't been said already? What could they add to such a statement, the alpha and the omega of the real world? Just as this Pathway was the summation of every other truth they had discussed, so too would their final statements wrap up everything they said or believed, all the dreams that had brought them to this table in the first place.

"I believe," the Psychologist said, "that our real, or true, self is healed because God created us perfect, and everything God created is eternal, not subject to disease and decay. We have chosen to look upon death instead of life, guilt instead of joy, and the world has reflected those decisions. But we were wrong in those decisions. It's really that simple. We were looking upon a world that didn't exist in reality, only in our dreams. Even the evidence that seemed to prove the existence of that world was suspect, because we always had the ability to choose how we would react to the circumstances we perceived."

"We have come to a very clear fork in the road," the Scientist said. "Most people will disagree with this statement, that the world is already healed. There is very little evidence, just as the Psychologist has just said, to back up this claim. And yet we seem to have entered a place where we don't need that kind of evidence. Once it becomes an experience, anchored in our souls and in the way we relate to one another, then it requires new eyes to see, eyes that see a New World."

"Yes," the Mystic added. "There is no way to explain this experience because it exists beyond words, beyond concepts. But when we have it, when it is full within us, then we don't need to explain. In fact, trying to explain it becomes pointless, because we can never get very close with words. But with our soul, yes, we can enter into it fully."

"This relates very directly to our modern science as well," the Scientist said. "What quantum science now suggests, and what the ancients said in the words of their day, is that all possibilities are already in existence. So for every instance of disease, illness and suffering, there exists an instance of peace, healing and youthful vitality. We determine which of these we experience in our conscious waking world by the choices we make, and how we address the challenges of our lives in every moment. So when we find ourselves choosing love and compassion, we attract healing energy into our lives, and that becomes part of the collective decision that determines what is happening in our world. Since in reality our world is already healed, we invite healing into our collective world as we demonstrate that healing in our lives."

"There are certainly parallel realities," the Psychologist said, "all existing at the same time in the same space, just as the Scientist said before. I liken it to having seven VCR's on top of a television set. Let's say that there are seven different programs playing, all showing a different movie. One is a masterpiece, one is boring, one is a tragedy, and so on, and our thoughts, feelings and emotions determine the one we decide to focus on. We push the button on the VCR that shows a particular show. Most people channel surf and have no sense of why the movie of their life is at one instant a tragedy and then a comedy. It's because they're pushing the button called 'fear'. But that masterpiece movie is always in there, always waiting to be viewed. Good doesn't have to be followed by bad. We can have a steady masterpiece if that's what we want. Also, I find that many people have the mistaken belief that they must grow through pain, or that God must test them. I believe we grow quicker through peace. We test ourselves, and God gave us the power to create our own tests."

"And why not draw tests into our lives that reflect joy instead of fear...?" the Mystic said.

"...Peace instead of war?" the Scientist added.

"Exactly... we can choose whatever reality we want. Isn't that the real foundation of this and every Pathway? We are not victims of the world, but we create it with every thought, feeling and emotion we experience."

"Yes," the Mystic said. "The world does not happen to us, but by us. We are co-creating our experience with the Mind we call God. We were never separate from that Mind except in our imaginations. But what was imagined is not real. Only the eternal is real... and that is our ultimate salvation."

"Science, Psychology and Mysticism are all saying the same thing," concluded the Scientist. "The world is already healed when we allow ourselves to experience that healing. It always comes back to us... to our perception of the world, of ourselves and of the reality many of us call God. When we understand these things, not with our minds but with our whole selves, then we are truly free."

Section 3

Prayers
and
Meditations

S o, now that we have established what it means to "Pray Peace," how do we activate this powerful force and literally pray a new world into existence? We said at the very beginning of this book that you have the power to change the world, not in grandiose ways, but in ways that are so essential that we often miss our opportunity. The goal of this book is not to lay a foundation that cannot be built upon, but to offer a simple solution that can be experienced by everyone, regardless of their intellectual prowess. This is a way of praying that completely baffles the intellect, for it takes the innocence of a child to embark upon such a lofty quest as "healing the whole universe." Throw away ideas like, "Who am I...?" or "I never have been able to before." Such concepts are meaningless now. Now that you understand the true goal of prayer, and realize that the world is nothing more than the projection of your mind and imagination, then you can use this ancient technology to create the world you want rather than the world you no longer want. If that makes sense to you then you have come a very long way indeed. If you are willing to lay aside the 'reasonable logic' of the intellect and accept a notion that the mind is completely unable to comprehend, then nothing will be out of your reach.

You will find so many ways to "Pray Peace" in your life. The more creative you are the better. Use the "Seven Pathways to Peace" in whatever way makes sense to you. They are like seeds that when given the right nourishment sprout and grow on their own. The seed does not need to be shown what to do, its wisdom only needs to be watered and released. Once this power is welcomed into our lives then the rest is easy. You may choose to meditate with the Pathways, reading them one at a time and letting their innate wisdom seep into your open mind. What I offer now is but one suggestion, one way for you to lift the words off the page and integrate them into your life. Remember, you are being led to a place where you can make your own decisions, where you are expected to become a 'Spiritual Adult'. You are ready to adapt what is offered here in a way that works with your own unique insights and gifts. The Spirit of Truth trusts you! Isn't that a freeing thought? Now take that gift and run with it, pushing yourself to the very limits of your perceived universe. You may be amazed at your own strength and wisdom.

Before we begin, let me give you just a few guidelines. When working with the Pathways, in whatever way you choose, let these three ideas rest in the back of your mind:

1. The world you desire already exists. You do not need to create it so much as draw it into your conscious experience.

2. Do not try to change anything in the world. Seek rather to change your mind, becoming that which you seek, and then observe the miracle.

3. The highest expression of 'Universal Mind', otherwise known as God, is Peace. (Peace, in this context, is the same as Love.) We are not referring to the ego's version of peace, which is nothing more than the opposite of conflict, but the "peace that surpasseth understanding."

Use these truths as the benchmarks that guide your practicing. They are like the Three Pillars of Peace, inspiring the place in your soul that already understands the experience you seek. Once that has been awakened, then you will not need any of these concepts for you will be their living expression. But until then, let them be like loose feathers that float back and forth in front of you, gentle reminders of the truth within.

A Week For Peace

Let this be the week you choose to 'Pray Peace' into your life. Choose to spend seven days focusing on how you can extend this gift to your daily relationships, at your job, and in all the ordinary situations in which you find yourself. Peace comes not so much through extraordinary phenomena, but through what we see in front of us every day. That is the proving ground, for it is there that we find the strongest charge, the greatest challenge, and the fullest opportunity to live lives that reflect these principles.

Let each day of this week be a prayer. Let your life be the full expression of this prayer, and let each Pathway teach you the deeper meaning of peace. We are not seeking to understand another concept, but to come into direct contact with the reality that exists beyond all concepts. Commit yourself to just seven days lived in this open space, and let the reality you have avoided till now dawn upon your mind.

The Seven Pathways to Peace

You are always praying; thought itself is prayer.

Whatever you focus your mind on, increases.

To change the world, change your thoughts about the world.

If you want to experience peace – become peace.

Peace is always present, though it is sometimes hidden.

Love is the only force in the universe.

The world is already healed.

The First Pathway

"You are always praying; thought itself is prayer."

MORNING PRAYER:

"Beloved One, open my heart today so that I may perceive my constant prayers. My thoughts have made the world I see, and so it is mine to undo the world of conflict and despair, revealing a bright alternative where only love is real. I am aware of the ways I have limited myself and have projected those limitations onto the whole universe. And in so realizing this, I will learn to pray in a new way, releasing the power of my creative soul which desires only one thing – Peace. Fill me now with your fire, and help me be attentive to my own mind. Teach me how to pray, Beloved One."

DAILY PRACTICE:

As often as you can today, ask yourself this simple question: "What am I praying for this instant?" Become aware of the thoughts that were going through your mind in that moment. Was your mind focused on a blessing or a curse? Were you worried about the future or preoccupied with the past? Or was your heart centered on the present moment where all possibilities exist? Be honest with yourself. Only you will know the truth. Then, when you are aware of your thoughts, say to yourself:

"I am willing to 'Pray Peace' this and every moment.
Only then will I experience the gift
I am willing to give to everyone."

Let this be your mantra today, for the more willing you are to become aware of your thoughts, no matter how fearful, the easier it will be to transform them into thoughts that illumine the dark places of your mind. If you have a watch that you can program to beep once an hour this might be a helpful reminder. Or you may decide that whenever you hear a certain word, like your name, you will become aware of whatever it is you are thinking. Most importantly, don't fall into the trap of judging your thoughts as good or bad, right or wrong. For now just become aware, and then be willing to transform.

The Second Pathway

"Whatever you focus your mind on, increases."

MORNING PRAYER:

"Beloved One, I take full responsibility for my thoughts this day. They have established the world I see, and so they have the power to create a New World based upon reality rather than illusion. What I focus on increases, and so I focus on Peace. This is the law, and I recognize my responsibility in using this law to fulfill my destiny. My destiny is to realize that I am one with my Creator, and therefore possess the creative power of God. This has always been so, but I have chosen a shadow rather than the Real World. I will use that power now to Pray a world into existence where conflict is impossible and separation is a forgotten dream. I resolutely fix my attention upon compassion and peace. I focus my mind only on the gifts that flow from your Infinite Heart, Beloved One, for anything else is not worthy of me. I accept the power you have given my mind, and I use it now to create a New World.

DAILY PRACTICE:

Having realized the power of your mind and heart, we will practice using that force to create the world you desire. When you begin your day, choose a 'statement of intent' that will reflect your commitment to focus only on Peace. An example would be:

"I focus my attention on seeing only Peace this day,"

or,

"Today I will perceive the Peace that exists everywhere, regardless of outer appearances."

Once again, as often as you can, stop and say your 'statement of intent' with concentrated power. Then look around yourself and choose to see reality instead of illusion. If you look out upon the world and find yourself stuck in traffic, choose to use that moment as an opportunity to experience and share Peace. Maybe you will choose to say a short prayer that will honor everyone who has impacted your life today. If you see two people, maybe even yourself, engaged in an argument, choose to see the Peace that lies on the other side of that conflict, the reality that seems to be hidden from your sight. Focus on that reality and watch as it begins to increase. Whatever you see in front of you, search for Peace, even if it is hard to find. It is there. It is always there. It is ours but to find it, then focus our thoughts and feelings on it.

The Third Pathway

"To change the world, change your thoughts about the world."

MORNING PRAYER:

"Beloved One, give us one day of realizing how best to change the world. We accept that the world we perceive is nothing more than the projection of our thoughts, feelings and emotions. We made everything, and everything we experience we have asked for. The universe changes only when we focus on compassion and peace, rather than competition and war. We take full responsibility today for building a world that reflects your Divine Plan, the New World where reality is established in the minds and hearts of every being everywhere. Use us. We turn ourselves over to you, Beloved, to be the instruments through which healing is experienced. We hold nothing back, but lay ourselves upon your holy altar where you will teach us what we need to know. This is the day we begin afresh, led by your gentle hand into the truth."

DAILY PRACTICE:

Begin the day by realizing what your real goal is, the reason you were born into this world. You are here to be an instrument of Peace, a vehicle through which a New World of Peace can come into being. We have already accepted responsibility for creating the world we perceive. Now we must go a step further. Knowing that we are victims of nothing, we set out to establish the world we claim to want, a world based upon the reality of love rather than the illusion of fear. Awareness is everything at this point. During the last two days we have become aware of the thoughts we have and how they influence the world we perceive. Now we will begin the process of changing those thoughts to reflect the healing we desire.

As often as you can, triggered either by a word you choose or a watch that beeps periodically throughout the day, become aware of the thoughts that preoccupy your mind. If you become aware of a thought that promotes healing and unity say to yourself:

"These are the thoughts and emotions that heal the world."

This affirmation alone has the power to trigger even more healing thoughts. If, however, you become aware of a separating thought, one that promotes conflict rather than healing, say to yourself:

"I choose to see Peace in this situation."

This phrase is not designed to deny what is right in front of you, but to transform it. This is one of the most powerful uses of Prayer, to transmute separating energies to energies that unite and heal. The problem and the solution are both in your mind. Look there for change and nowhere else. Do this exercise as often as you can throughout the day.

The Fourth Pathway

"If you want to experience peace – become peace."

MORNING PRAYER:

"Beloved, there is only one thing in the universe that means anything to me now – Peace. It is the only thing that can satisfy my hunger and quench my thirst, and I am willing to learn the true path that leads to the fulfillment of this desire. I will become the experience I seek. I will give myself completely to the Peace my intellect cannot understand. I willingly lay aside everything that does not correspond to this perfect reality and choose to adopt any position that will lead me to the truth. I am that Peace now. I will look past all the forces that seem to block me from accessing this holy temple and perceive myself as already whole, and I will perceive all beings everywhere in the same Light. I will not accept anything less than the perfection of your Grace, Beloved One, and I commit myself to sharing that same Grace with everyone."

DAILY PRACTICE:

How does one become Peace? Since every thought is a prayer, then it is through our thoughts, feelings and emotions that we unlock the door that leads to everything we desire. There is nothing new or revolutionary about this statement. It is, in fact, all we have ever done. The difference is that we now choose to become an instrument of Peace rather than conflict, and the world will certainly reflect this new choice. The world waits upon our command, and then it responds according to our focused desire. We have been taught that we cannot control the world but are controlled by it, and all evidence seems to support this premise. But we will now look to a deeper reality that cannot be understood by the mind. We admit that these ideas mean very little to the intellect, but they are real nonetheless. It is through 'Praying Peace' that we realize the truth that is hidden to the intellect, and then we will know that we are one with that truth.

We cannot become Peace without the assistance of the Spirit of Peace. In other words, we must look to God to teach us everything we need to know. We have forgotten what it feels like to live in this bright reality all the time, and it is through surrender that we begin to remember again. Let this be a day of quiet prayer. Ask for help in whatever way feels comfortable for you, and listen for the answer. Stop as often as you can and give yourself to the Teacher that leads to the truth. And trust everything that is revealed, for this Teacher shares your goal, that of becoming Peace.

The Fifth Pathway

"Peace is always present,
though it is sometimes hidden."

MORNING PRAYER:

"Beloved One, Help me learn this essential lesson today. Teach me how to look past the conflict that seems to exist in the world and perceive the Peace that is always present. Whenever the world attempts to prove that war can eclipse Peace, let me go within to the heart that comprehends reality. Then I will know the truth, the truth that can't be seen by human eyes, but which can be experienced by the soul. Peace is present even where conflict seems to rule. Teach me this law that I may learn to see with spiritual eyes, eyes that see only the truth. Inspire that place within me that sees past the illusions of the ego and perceives the Peace that you never lose sight of."

DAILY PRACTICE:

Look into as many eyes as you can today, and ask to see the truth within them. You will be amazed at how much you can learn by looking into someone's eyes and not judging them. And the gift you give will surely be received by you as well. It will be easy to see Peace in the eyes of many of those you choose today, and it may be harder to see it in others. These are the people who offer you the greatest opportunity to learn the lessons that will set you free. Look at them and try to suspend your judgment or fear. Look past all those illusions and ask to see the real face that lies behind the mask. We all wear masks, but it is ours to see past them to the place where we are the same, the face of holiness itself. Look for that face everywhere today, as often as you can. Maybe you can set a goal for yourself, to look into the eyes of at least one person an hour and see the truth. The more you do this, the more you will feel the Real World. That, after all, is the goal of all these exercises.

The Sixth Pathway

"Love is the only force in the universe."

MORNING MEDITATION:

"Beloved One, I choose to perceive the one law that exists in reality today. There is only one force in the universe, and it is love. What else do I need to learn but the law that will set me free? Every lesson to which I have opened my mind has led to this quiet place where my mind can rest and where I discover the true meaning of Peace. If love is the only true force in the universe then fear must be an illusion, as well as everything that arises from fear. This truth is my salvation, and it is in living this truth that I become a Peacemaker. This is the day I will release all illusions and accept the truth. This is the moment I surrender all my defenses to the truth and willingly offer you a place in my heart to live and grow. I will seek only love today, Beloved One, for it is the only thing that makes sense to me now."

DAILY PRACTICE:

We have now come to the point in our growth where we can see love everywhere, including the places where it did not seem to exist before. In the past we learned to differentiate between what would nurture us and what would threaten our lives, the difference between love and fear. But we have come to higher ground now, a place where we can see so much further than before. And what is the one law we perceive when we ascend this mountain? Only love, for it is truly the only active, real force in the universe. We will rest there for a moment and watch the movements of love that evaded our attention till now. We will look out upon the world and see the bright shining light of love as it activates our higher centers of awareness, reminding us that God has never once lost this focus, not even for an instant.

Spend the day quietly reflecting upon this new perspective you have gained. As you go about the ordinary routines that define who you think you are, look out at everyone you meet and let them teach you who you really are. Let them reflect the truth in you, not the illusion, and watch as this wave of love washes you clean. Learn to look past what 'seems' to be happening to what truth would reveal. When you happen upon a situation that seems conflictive or dangerous, look with the eyes of compassion upon everyone involved and let your sight transform everything you perceive. You do not need to say a word, for your presence will be enough. The reality of love is never threatened by these dramas, but you must open yourself to this reality if you are to experience it for yourself. Let this be the day you choose love, resolutely, seeing it everywhere you look. Be very quiet today and let love teach you its single lesson – that God has not forgotten you, but has held you safe from the illusions that seem to upset your balance.

The Seventh Pathway

"The world is already healed."

MORNING PRAYER:

"Beloved One, I have come to the point now where I can see the truth that I have hidden from till now. I tried to create a world that did not coincide with your Divine Plan. I tried to create an opposite for love, and give peace an alternative. But none of these things were heard by you, and you held the truth safe, protecting reality from the illusions that I would use to destroy the truth. I now lay down my sword and accept what you have revealed to me. The world is already healed, and I choose to look upon this truth today. Where once I saw an attack, I will now look upon the truth. Where once I saw hatred, I will choose only love, for that is what you have chosen for me, Beloved One. I will offer you all the illusions that have separated me from this vision of holiness, and I will trust you in everything. Love has chosen me, and I do now respond. Hold me in your arms that I may feel the grace that flows from your heart into mine, now and always."

DAILY PRACTICE:

Today we will take our daily practice to the final point. This is the art of spiritual peacemaking, the realization that regardless of how things appear, the world is already healed. Does this make sense to the one who looks with their eyes upon the world of conflict and war? Such a statement is insane to anyone who uses their eyes to judge. We have now learned that the physical eyes cannot see reality, but only the shadow of reality, the world based upon fear. We must look with spiritual eyes if we are to see the truth, eyes that see everything as the same, blanketed in holiness and grace. We realize that there is only one law that is active in our lives, the law of peace, or love. Anything that seems to oppose this law is an illusion and isn't real. When we focus our vision in this way then we become the peacemakers we long to be, for we allow the miracle to work through us. We cannot know what the miracle is or how it works. We can only become that miracle, and let the world transform around us.

Let today's Pathway be your mantra today. As you go through your day, look with loving eyes upon the world and say, "The world is already healed." You are being called to witness this healing. When you witness in this way then you empower the transformation of the universe into truth, becoming the vehicle and instrument through which peace is extended in the world. As often as you think, stop and look around you, then say the Pathway with as much gratitude as you can feel. This is the key, for gratitude is the catalyst that activates the Real World. Use it as your only tool today. The words you speak are true, and the truth will lead you into an experience that completely transcends the intellect. The mind has now found its place behind the heart, and we step forward with spirits filled with love. You have come a very long way indeed, but you are home now. You are the eyes that look out upon a healed world. Blessed be those who allow themselves to be used in this way.

Prayers

Many of us have been taught to believe that the words we speak define our prayers. We were given a list of prayers to say before we went to sleep, or when we were in church with our family. Now we understand that the words we say are of little importance without the emotions and feelings that give them power. Words can certainly trigger a place within us that responds to the more subtle energies where prayer becomes a real, active force in our lives, but it is really the feelings they inspire that have the magic. Without the emotions and feelings the prayer sits upon the ground and does not move.

The Prayers that are offered here have been a very important part of my own journey because they have triggered within me the feeling of peace. I have traveled around the world performing the peace prayers from the twelve major religions of the world, and they have transformed my life, not because there is any special power in the words themselves, but because they remind me of the thing that is most important in my life. I would like to offer them now to you, the reader of this book, in the hope that they will touch that same place in your heart. You may want to picture someone from each of these religions when you pray each prayer, or whatever you need to do to trigger the emotion of peace that is the real goal. I cannot tell you what to do, for we will all access the feeling of peace in whatever way is most natural to us. Experiment with them until they find a way into your heart.

These prayers were first prayed together on November 11, 1986, when the leaders of the major religions of the world came together in Assisi, Italy, to focus on peace. We honor these leaders now as we ask to be used to create a world based upon the laws of love.

Hindu Prayer for Peace

Note: "Shanti" is the ancient Sanskrit word for the "Peace which surpasseth understanding."

Oh God, lead us from the unreal to the Real
Oh God, lead us from darkness to light
Oh God, lead us from death to immortality
Shanti, Shanti, Shanti unto all.

Oh Lord God almighty, may there be peace in Celestial
  regions.
May there be peace on earth
May the waters be appeasing
May herbs be wholesome, and may trees and plants
  bring peace to all.
May all beneficent beings bring peace to us
May thy Vedic Law propagate peace all through the
  world.

May all things be a source of peace to us
And may thy peace itself bestow peace on all
And may that peace come to me also.

Buddhist Prayer for Peace

May all beings everywhere
plagued with sufferings of body and mind
quickly be freed from their illnesses.
May those frightened cease to be afraid
and may those bound be free.
May the powerless find power,
and may people think of befriending one another.
May those who find themselves in trackless,
fearful wildernesses – the children, the aged,
the unprotected – be guarded by beneficent
    celestials,
and may they quickly attain Buddhahood.

Zoroastrian Prayer for Peace

We pray to God to eradicate all the
misery in the world:
that understanding triumph over ignorance,
that generosity triumph over indifference,
that trust triumph over contempt, and
that truth triumph over falsehood.

Janist Prayer for Peace

Note: "Dharma" translates as "essential quality or character."

Peace and Universal Love is the essence
of the Gospel preached by all the
Enlightened Ones.
The Lord has preached that equanimity
is the Dharma.
Forgive do I creatures all,
and let all creatures forgive me.
Unto all have I amity, and unto none enmity.
Know that violence is the root cause of all miseries in
    the world.
Violence, in fact, is the knot of bondage.
"Do not injure any living being."
This is the eternal, perennial, and unalterable
way of spiritual life.
A weapon, howsoever powerful it may be,
can always be superseded by a superior one;
but no weapon can, however,
be superior to non-violence and love.

Jewish Prayer for Peace

Come, let us go up to the mountain of
the Lord, that we may walk the
paths of the Most High.
And we shall beat our swords into ploughshares,
and our spears into pruning hooks.
Nation shall not lift up sword against nation –
neither shall they learn war any more.
And none shall be afraid, for the mouth of the
Lord of Hosts has spoken.

Shinto Prayer for Peace

Although the people living
across the ocean
surrounding us, I believe,
are all our brothers and sisters,
why are there constant troubles in this world?
Why do winds and waves rise in the
ocean surrounding us?
I only earnestly wish that the wind will
soon puff away all the clouds which are
hanging over the tops of the mountains.

Native African Prayer for Peace

Almighty God, the Great
Thumb we cannot evade to
tie any knot;
the Roaring Thunder that splits
mighty trees;
the all-seeing Lord up on high who sees
even the footprints of an antelope on
a rock mass here on Earth.
You are the one who does
not hesitate to respond to our call.
You are the cornerstone of peace.

Native American Prayer for Peace

O Great Spirit of our
Ancestors, I raise
my pipe to you;
To your messengers the four winds, and
to Mother Earth who provides
for your children.
Give us the wisdom to teach our children
to love, to respect, and to be kind
to each other, so that they may grow
with peace in mind.
Let us learn to share all good things that
you provide for us on this Earth.

Muslim Prayer for Peace

In the name of Allah
the beneficent, the merciful.
Praise be to the Lord of the
Universe who has created us and
made us into tribes and nations
that we may know each other, not that
we may despise each other.
If the enemy incline towards peace, do
thou also incline towards peace, and
trust God, for the Lord is the one that
heareth and knoweth all things.
And the servants of God,
most Gracious are those who walk on
the Earth in humility, and when we
address them, we say "PEACE"

Baha'i Prayer for Peace

Be generous in prosperity
and thankful in adversity,
Be fair in thy judgment,
and guarded in thy speech.
Be a lamp unto those who walk
in darkness, and a home
to the stranger.
Be eyes to the blind, and a guiding light
unto the feet of the erring.
Be a breath of life to the body of
humankind, a dew to the soil of
the human heart,
and a fruit upon the tree of humility.

Sikh Prayer for Peace

God adjudges us according
to our deeds,
not the coat that we wear:
that truth is above everything,
but higher still is truthful living.
Know that we attain God when we love,
and only that victory
endures in consequence of which no
one is defeated.

Christian Prayer for Peace

Blessed are the PEACEMAKERS
for they shall be known as
the Children of God.
But I say to you that hear, love your enemies,
do good to those who hate you,
bless those who curse you,
pray for those who abuse you.
To those who strike you on the cheek,
offer the other also,
and from those who take away your cloak,
do not withhold your coat as well.
Give to everyone who begs from you,
and of those who take away your goods,
do not ask them again.
And as you wish that others would do to you,
do so to them.

Finally, I would like to offer this shortened version of the peace prayers that can be easily memorized and prayed in a few moments. It is a perfect prayer to add to a service, or to offer on your own. Also, you can find all these prayers on a new CD called *Ecclesia Volume 1* produced by Etherean Music, which you can listen to in conjunction with this book. You can buy the CD in stores or you can go to EmissaryofLight.com and order online.

Sacred Office of Peace

Hindu Prayer

Oh God, Lead us from the unreal to the real.
Oh God, lead us from darkness into light.
Oh God, lead us from death to immortality.
Shanti, Shanti, Shanti unto all.

Buddhist Prayer

May all beings everywhere plagued of sufferings of body and
    mind,
quickly be freed from their illnesses.
May all beings swiftly attain Buddhahood.

Zoroastrian Prayer

We pray to God that understanding will triumph over
    ignorance,
that generosity will triumph over indifference,
that trust will triumph over contempt,
and that truth will triumph over falsehood.

Janist Prayer

Peace and universal love is the essence of all the Gospels.
Forgive do I creatures all,
and let all creatures forgive me.

Jewish Prayer

Oh come let us go up to the mountain of the Lord,
that we may walk the paths of the Most High.
And we will beat our swords into ploughshares
and our spears into pruning hooks.

Shinto Prayer

We earnestly wish that the wind will soon puff away
all the clouds hanging over the tops of the mountains.

Native African Prayer

For you are the one who does not hesitate to respond to our
   call,
you are the cornerstone of peace.

Native American Prayer

Give us the wisdom to teach our children to love,
to respect and to be kind to one another,
that we may grow with peace in mind.

Muslim Prayer

Praise be to the Lord of the Universe,
who has created us and made us into tribes and nations
that we may know each other,
not despise each other.

Baha'i Prayer

Be a breath of life unto the body of human kind,
a dew upon the human heart,
and a fruit upon the tree of humility.

Sikh Prayer

Know that we attain God when we love,
and only that victory endures in consequence of which
no one is defeated.

Christian Prayer

Love your enemies,
do good to those who hate you,
bless those who curse you,
pray for those who abuse you.
Blessed be the Peacemakers,
for they shall be called the Children of God.

FINDHORN Press

Findhorn Press is the publishing business of the Findhorn Community which has grown around the Findhorn Foundation in northern Scotland.

For further information about the Findhorn Foundation and the Findhorn Community, please contact:

Findhorn Foundation

The Visitors Centre
The Park, Findhorn IV36 3TY, Scotland, UK
tel 01309 690311• fax 01309 691301
email reception@findhorn.org
www.findhorn.org

For a complete Findhorn Press catalogue, please contact:

Findhorn Press

The Park, Findhorn,
Forres IV36 3TY
Scotland, UK
Tel 01309 690582
freephone 0800-389-9395
Fax 01309 690036

P. O. Box 13939
Tallahassee
Florida 32317-3939, USA
Tel (850) 893 2920
toll-free 1-877-390-4425
Fax (850) 893 3442

e-mail info@findhornpress.com
www.findhornpress.com